NOMADS OF EURASIA

Natural History Museum of Los Angeles County

Academy of Sciences of the U.S.S.R.

NOMADS
OF EURASIA

edited by
VLADIMIR N. BASILOV

translation by
MARY FLEMING ZIRIN

photography by
DANA LEVY AND JOEL SACKETT

NATURAL HISTORY MUSEUM OF LOS ANGELES COUNTY
in association with
UNIVERSITY OF WASHINGTON PRESS
SEATTLE AND LONDON

Published in conjunction with the exhibit
Nomads: Masters of the Eurasian Steppe

Natural History Museum of Los Angeles County
Los Angeles, California
February–April 1989

Denver Museum of Natural History
Denver, Colorado
June–September 1989

U.S. National Museum of Natural History
Smithsonian Institution, Washington, D.C.
November 1989–February 1990

The Natural History Museum of Los Angeles County
is indebted to the lenders to the exhibition:

Hermitage, Leningrad (GE)

State Museum of Ethnography, Leningrad (GME)

Institute of Ethnography, Moscow and Leningrad (IE)

Institute of History, Archaeology, and Ethnography,
Kazakh Academy of Sciences, Alma-Ata (IIAE)

Institute of History, Philology, and Philosophy,
Siberian Division, Novosibirsk (IIFF)

Peter the Great's Museum of Anthropology and
Ethnography, Leningrad (MAE)

Museum of the History of Religion and Atheism,
Leningrad (MIRA)

State Museum of the Tuva A.S.S.R., Kyzyl (TRM)

The exhibition was made possible by
the leadership gift of

Occidental Petroleum Corporation

with additional support from

Max Baril

The California Council for the Humanities,
a state program of the
National Endowment for the Humanities

The University of Washington Press
The National Endowment for the Humanities

Natural History Museum of Los Angeles County
Los Angeles, California 90007

LC 88-063441

ISBN-0-295-96816-8 softcover
ISBN-0-295-96815-X hardcover

Distributed by
The University of Washington Press
P.O. Box C50096
Seattle, Washington 98145-5096

Cover: Buryats, early twentieth century.

Contents

PAGES V–VIII, LEFT TO RIGHT
Buryat woman. 1905. **Yakut woman.** Early twentieth century. **Turkic monument.** Barlyk steppes. **Uzbek costume.** Modeled by N. Shakhanova, 1988. **Tuvinian man.** Early twentieth century. **Turkmen woman.** 1908. **Teleut woman.** 1930s. **Turkmen girl.** 1969. **Khakass man.** Early twentieth century.

Foreword

Over the past 3,000 years, nomadic peoples inhabited the Eurasian steppes from the northern shores of the Black Sea to the Altai region, Tuva, and Mongolia. From the early part of the first millennium B.C. the nomads practiced animal husbandry, devising forms of culture particularly suited to the conditions of their mobile way of life and the demands of their fragile economy. Saddle and stirrup originated among these peoples, and they developed clothing suited for a life spent in the saddle, an easily transportable home–the yurt, and distinctive food products based on mares' milk. Powerful nomadic kingdoms arose repeatedly from the earliest times into the Middle Ages to assume dominion over the known world, and the names of their dynamic leaders–Chingis-khan, Khubilai-khan, and Attila–are still synonymous with brilliance in military and administrative strategy. Less well known is the nomads' role in linking the developing civilizations of East and West and their lasting contributions to world culture in general.

This book is published in conjunction with the presentation in 1989 of the first comprehensive exhibit on the Eurasian nomads to be organized for the United States. The book and the exhibition, Nomads: Masters of the Eurasian Steppe, are the products of a collaboration between the Academy of Sciences of the

U.S.S.R. and the Natural History Museum of Los Angeles County. More than 1,200 artifacts from eight major archaeological and ethnographic institutions of the Soviet Union will first be on exhibit in our museum in Los Angeles. The show is then traveling to the Denver Museum of Natural History and concludes its tour at the U.S. National Museum of Natural History, Smithsonian Institution, in Washington, D.C. Peter C. Keller, Associate Director for Public Programs at our museum, established the concept for the U.S. tour of the exhibit. Andrei P. Kapitsa, Deputy Secretary General of the U.S.S.R. Academy of Sciences, provided overall direction for the Soviet arrangements. The U.S. tour has been made possible through the efforts of John G. Welles, Director of the Denver Museum of Natural History, and Frank H. Talbot, Director of the U.S. National Museum of Natural History.

At the heart of the exhibition are archaeological and ethnographic materials from the collections of Peter the Great's Museum of Anthropology and Ethnography, the Leningrad division of the Institute of Ethnography of the U.S.S.R. Academy of Sciences. Other objects—many on public display for the first time—have been contributed by the Hermitage, Leningrad; the Archaeological Museum of the Institute of History, Archaeology, and Ethnography of the Kazakh Academy of Sciences, Alma-Ata; the Moscow Division of the Institute of Ethnography; the Institute of History, Philology, and Philosophy, Siberian Division of the U.S.S.R. Academy of Sciences, Novosibirsk; the State Museum of Ethnography, Leningrad; the State Museum of the Tuva A.S.S.R., Kyzyl; and the Museum of the History of Religion and Atheism, Leningrad. We are indebted to the directors of these Soviet institutions for making their priceless collections available to the exhibition; in particular we thank Karl M. Baipakov of the Kazakh Academy of Sciences, Rudolf F. Its of Peter the Great's Museum, and Boris Piotrovskii of the Hermitage for facilitating photography of artifacts from their institutions.

The exhibit and the book reflect the most recent research of a group of distinguished Soviet ethnographers, historians, and archaeologists, headed by Vladimir N. Basilov of the Institute of Ethnography in Moscow. Dr. Basilov has worked tirelessly as curator of the exhibit and editor of this book to make the complex history of the nomads accessible to the American public. His vast knowledge of the cultures of the steppes is reflected in the drama and coherence of the exhibit and in the painstaking scholarship of the book.

The first gift in support of Nomads: Masters of the Eurasian Steppe has been provided by Occidental Petroleum Corporation. Additional support has been received from Max Baril, the California Council for the Humanities, and the University of Washington Press. We are grateful for these generous gifts.

The Natural History Museum of Los Angeles County has found its collaboration with the U.S.S.R. Academy of Sciences to be extremely rewarding. The Nomads exhibit and book celebrate the wisdom, accomplishments, and endurance of an ancient people and provide exuberant testimony to the diversity of life in the vast Union of Soviet Socialist Republics.

I thank everyone who contributed to the realization of this exciting project.

CRAIG C. BLACK
Director
Natural History Museum of Los Angeles County

The public role of the humanities and social sciences includes not only research into various aspects of life, but also dissemination of scientific knowledge. Exhibitions that deal with the history and culture of the peoples of our world are an effective way of making knowledge accessible. The visitor is attracted by the exhibits, history is presented graphically, and scientific concepts are reflected in actual images from the past.

History is a field that has not only cognitive interest but also practical value, because it can enrich our understanding of the contemporary world. Today's world grew out of preceding civilizations; the past helps us to experience the present more profoundly. But perhaps the chief practical significance of history is that it teaches us to think more flexibly and broadly. History makes clear that different cultures were created by societies living under different conditions and that, just like our culture, they had their virtues and shortcomings. Moreover, cultural differences promoted social progress. History teaches us to avoid narrow, partisan judgments of ways of life and ideas unlike our own—and that is exactly what we need today. The ability to understand others' values is at present an important positive force in political thought.

Nomadism, the subject of this book and the exhibit it accompanies, is sometimes seen as a primitive, backward phenomenon that retarded the development of civilization. This is an oversimplification based on imperfect knowledge of the facts. The nomadic animal herders worked out effective adaptations to their natural surroundings and created an original culture. Some of their cultural achievements were imitated by sedentary peoples. Nomadism as a whole was such a significant historical phenomenon that we cannot fully understand the history of the many countries and peoples of Eurasia over the last three millennia without taking it into account. In the Soviet Union the nomads settled into sedentary life soon after the revolution, but many of their ancestors' traditions are preserved in their daily life and remain an organic part of their contemporary culture.

The goal of the exhibition is to display the colorful and distinctive cultures of the nomadic herders who lived in the steppes, deserts, and semideserts of Eurasia from the first millennium B.C. Their original way of life was connected with their mobility and the necessity of driving their animals from pasture to pasture. The nomads developed horse harness and weaponry and furthered the wide use of the rigid saddle, stirrups, and saber. They invented various kinds of mobile dwelling—from frame houses on wheels to the collapsible yurt—and made trousers a garment for daily wear. They devised various ways of processing milk products and used lightweight leather vessels. The history of the fiddle begins in the nomad world. The basic traits of nomadic culture did not develop all at once; many traditions have been repeatedly transformed.

The items in the exhibit reflect the complex path of development of the nomadic peoples' cultures. Visitors will see objects typical of the life of the nomads both in times far removed from our days and in the recent past. These objects have come from various U.S.S.R. museums.

The main organizer of Nomads: Masters of the Eurasian Steppe is the Institute of Ethnography of the U.S.S.R. Academy of Sciences, which includes the oldest museum in the country, the Museum of Anthropology and Ethnography named for and founded by Peter the Great in 1714. With a few exceptions, the objects on exhibit have never been seen in the New World, and some of them—recent archaeological finds—have never been shown in the U.S.S.R. The exhibit has already traveled to Japan, Finland, and Sweden; it has been considerably expanded for display in the United States.

Permit me wholeheartedly to welcome visitors to the exhibit. I am sure that it can only serve to strengthen mutual understanding and friendship between the Soviet and American peoples.

P. N. Fedoseev
Vice-President, Academy of Sciences
of the U.S.S.R.

Preface

Vladimir N. Basilov received expert assistance in selecting and preparing objects for exhibition and photography from Kemal A. Akishev, Marianna G. Antons, Karl M. Baipakov, Rosa B. Bektureeva, Sabir B. Faradzhev, E. G. Fëdorova, Vladimir A. Kinchikov, V. D. Kubarev, Vladimir A. Lamin, T. Ch. Norbu, Larisa R. Pavlinskaya, Ol'ga N. Panarina, and T. A. Popova.

The descriptions of illustrations in the book were written by Kemal A. Akishev, Karl M. Baipakov, Vladimir N. Basilov, Vladimir I. D'yachenko, Vera P. D'yakonova, Mikhail V. Gorelik, Mark G. Kramarovskii, Zh. K. Kurmankulov, Vadim P. Kurylëv, Nina P. Loba-chëva, Evgenii I. Lubo-Lesnichenko, Ol'ga B. Naumova, Larisa R. Pavlinskaya, R. R. Rakhimov, Georgii N. Simakov, N. Zh. Shakhanova, Sev'yan I. Vainshtein, and Natal'ya L. Zhukovskaya.

Mary F. Zirin translated the text and provided hours of research on the pertinent literature. The translation involved transliteration of terms for articles that cover nearly three millennia and a wide diversity of subjects and terms from nearly a score of languages belonging to four major families (Indo-European, Ural-Altaic, Semitic, and Sino-Tibetan). In general, technical words in these languages are given in forms used by Western scholars in the field or dictionary citations (i.e., the equivalent of nom. s.). Proper and geographical names are from standard English reference sources. Russian-English transliteration is American Standard (note that Cyrillic letters in artifact accession numbers have been transliterated), and Chinese references follow Wade-Giles. The Central Asian languages are in the transliterated spellings recommended by Allworth, 1971:295–387.

The list of additional literature includes books in English that the translator and reviewers found useful as well as publications and articles recommended by the Soviet authors.

Elizabeth J. W. Barber, Donald Chaput, Daniel M. Cohen, Ralph Leighton, Gary Seaman, and Mary F. Zirin made valuable comments on the manuscript. Margaret Ann Hardin provided expert advice on a number of points relating to the manuscript's editing and review. The book was designed by Dana Levy; Letitia Burns O'Connor coordinated production in the U.S. and the Orient.

The design and installation of the exhibition, production of publications, and arrangements for the United States tour were coordinated by the Natural History Museum of Los Angeles County, under the direction of Craig C. Black. Mark A. Rodriguez supervised protocol preparations and other diplomatic arrangements necessary for production of the exhibition and associated publications. James D. Olson designed the exhibit; Janet L. Davidson coordinated the details of the U.S. tour; Kathleen L. Rydar supervised funding of the project, Susan E. Crow prepared proposals for government grants, and John Charnay sought gifts from individual and corporate donors. Lella F. Smith directed handling and condition-reporting of objects; Mary Ann Dunn developed the public relations campaign; Richard Owston supervised construction in the exhibit halls; Shelley Stephens supervised design and production of the exhibition poster; and Joan C. Grasty coordinated the museum's related education programming. Harold and Erica Van Pelt provided special photographs for the exhibition.

A symposium, Ecology and Empire: Nomads in the Cultural Evolution of the Old World, was held at the University of Southern California and the Natural History Museum in February 1989; a number of Soviet and North American scholars presented papers at the symposium, which was organized by J. Stephen Lansing, Gary Seaman, and Andre Singer, all of the university's Department of Anthropology. The symposium was one of a number of events for the academic community and the general public held in conjunction with the exhibition.

Richard Feynman and Ralph Leighton originally brought the Nomads exhibition to the museum's attention. Prof. Feynman's enthusiasm for a U.S. showing of the Soviet materials was a key factor in the initial discussions about the exhibition and symposium. Ralph Leighton acted as special advisor for the exhibition and was involved in many stages of its planning and installation. Arrangements for the appearance of the exhibit in Denver and Washington, D.C., were coordinated by Alan Espenlaub (Denver Museum of Natural History) and Sheila Mutchler and Marjorie Stoller (U.S. National Museum of Natural History).

Lella F. Smith, Dana Levy, Joel Sackett, and I were assisted in our work and treated to gracious hospitality in the Soviet Union by Karl A. Akishev, Marianna G. Antons, Sofia P. Babkina, Rosa Bektureeva, Sabir B. Faradzhev, Vladimir A. Kinchikov, Mark G. Kramarovskii, Vadim P. Kurylëv, Galina V. Lebedinskaya, Evgenii I. Lubo-Lesnichenko, Ol'ga N. Panarina, Larisa R. Pavlinskaya, Sergei N. Polyakov, Rakhman Rakhimov, Nurilya Zh. Shakhanova, and Vitali A. Suslov.

The history of the nomadic and seminomadic peoples of Eurasia is replete with innovation and achievement and is characterized by material cultures of striking originality and beauty. The work of bringing images of these dynamic people to a new audience in the United States has been very gratifying for everyone involved.

ROBIN A. SIMPSON
Head of Publications
Natural History Museum of Los Angeles County

NOMADS OF EURASIA

Introduction

Vladimir N. Basilov

Over a period of nearly three thousand years (from the beginning of the first millennium B.C.) the nomads of the steppes inhabited vast territories from the northern shores of the Black Sea to the northern borders of China. Nomadism was a mobile way of life closely connected to economic circumstances, since it was economic necessity that forced people to migrate from place to place. The nomads of the Eurasian steppes were mostly engaged in extensive livestock herding. When their animals had devoured all the forage in one pasture area, they were driven to feed in another.

Nomadism had a marked seasonal character because in many cases the pastures on which the livestock could live during the summer months were not suitable for winter—and vice versa. The extent of migration was different for different peoples, and it is evidently impossible to find any regular pattern overall that fits all nomads. William of Rubruck, a thirteenth-century traveler, reported that "[the Mongols] drive their cattle to graze on the pasture lands without water in winter when there is snow there, for the snow provides them with water." But he also noted that "in winter they come down to the warmer districts in the south, in summer they go up to the cooler ones in the north" (Rubruck, 1955:94). In the eighteenth and nineteenth centuries, considerable numbers of the Kazakhs also migrated with their livestock to the south before the onslaught of winter, and then in the spring headed back. But some Turkmenian groups who

lived in the environs of the Balkhan Mountains took their herds to winter in the north, deep in the Karakum desert. There they found sufficient quantities of forage and snow, and the dunes protected the animals from the cold wind. There were some groups of nomads, living near or in the middle of the mountains, who drove their livestock to high pastures for the summer; others, on the contrary, pastured at high altitudes in the winter. Even into the Middle Ages, some Mongols spent their summers in the mountains (Polo, 1984:55). The nomads who lived by the Caspian sea "go south in the winter towards the sea, and in the summer they go up north along the banks of the same rivers to the mountains" (Plano Carpini, 1955:55). Many of the Kirghiz from ancient times set out with their herds to high alpine meadows when spring came, returning to the valleys for the winter. But in the nineteenth century the favorite winter area for part

Kazakhs milking sheep. Early twentieth century. Photograph courtesy of Peter the Great's Museum of Anthropology and Ethnography, Leningrad.

<small>OPPOSITE</small>
Tuvinians. Early twentieth century. Photograph courtesy of Peter the Great's Museum of Anthropology and Ethnography, Leningrad.

<small>PAGE XVI</small>
Kazakhs. Early twentieth century. Photograph courtesy of Peter the Great's Museum of Anthropology and Ethnography, Leningrad.

of the eastern Kazakhs was the mountains. Most of the Tuvinians arranged to spend their winters in the mountains (Vainshtein, 1972:66). Forage was accessible to the livestock in winter pastures in open spots (in particular, on mountain slopes), where the snow cover was brushed away by winds, facilitating the animals' search for grass.

The routes of migration were therefore determined by the presence of pastures suitable for livestock grazing. At different times of the year these pastures could be found in different spots. The migrations took many circumstances into account. In central and northern Mongolia, for example, the herders gathered for the summer around rivers and lakes. But in southwest Turkmenia, during the summer the herders abandoned the banks of the Atrek River where gadflies and mosquitoes harassed them. Kara-kalpak herders also brought their herds to the banks of the Amudar'ya and the Sea of Aral only in autumn; it was too damp for sheep in the summers.

The availability of pasture also affected the distances the nomads traveled. In the eighteenth and nineteenth centuries some groups of Kazakhs migrated over distances of 1,000–1,500 kilometers. For the Turkmens in the nineteenth century the distances between seasonal pastures were rarely greater than 20–25 kilometers, and the range of the Altaians' migrations rarely exceeded 10 kilometers. Radloff considered that

there was no true migration in the Altai, since there was sufficient forage everywhere (Radloff, 1884:1:286).

How often the herders moved from place to place during a single season also depended on the condition of the pastures. Many nomads stayed in the same place all winter. But this was far from being the general rule. Nineteenth-century Mongols, for instance, migrated even in winter, although less frequently and over shorter distances than during the summer. The Altaians and Tuvinians also often moved about during the winter, traveling only a few kilometers away from the previous camp.

Natural conditions also influenced the composition of the herd. The favorite animals of the nomads of the Eurasian steppes were sheep, horses, and camels, all of which could easily withstand long migrations. Sheep and goats were found everywhere, although the latter were much less abundant, but raising horses in herds proved possible only in limited areas. For instance, although the Turkmens were famous for raising excellent riding horses (the Akhal-teke breed), they did not keep them in herds because only sheep, goats, and camels could feed on their desert pastures. The breeding of camels—strong, undemanding animals useful for carrying heavy loads—also received differing emphasis among different groups of herders. In the late nineteenth and early twentieth centuries, camel-raising, along with sheep-raising, was a leading sector of the Turkmenian economy, and was also important for the Kazakhs, in particular, those who inhabited the southern part of the Kazakh steppes. On the other hand, according to the 1931 census, barely more than one percent of Tuvinian herders owned camels.

Cattle also played a substantial role in the life of the nomads. Over 2,000 years ago, the Scythians were already harnessing oxen to their wagons. However, cattle could be raised only in areas with sufficient grass and water. The nomadic Turkmenian herders did not keep cows at all, and the Kazakhs kept few cows even in the nineteenth century, except in certain regions where pastures were ample enough for cattle-raising. But from 1931 census data, we find that the Tuvinians had more cattle than horses. The Mongols raised cattle both in medieval and modern times, although the proportion varied from place to place. Yaks were raised from ancient times in a number of regions of Tuva, the Altai, Kirghizia, and Mongolia.

The attachment of the clans or tribes to their migrational territory depended also on securing pastures. Among the thirteenth-century Mongols, Rubruck reported, "every captain knows... the limits of his pasturage and where to feed his flocks winter, summer, spring and autumn" (Rubruck, 1955:94). Among the Kirghiz in the

Buryats. Early twentieth century. Photograph courtesy of Peter the Great's Museum of Anthropology and Ethnography, Leningrad.

nineteenth century "each tribe and clan migrated within a fixed territory" (Abramson, 1971:72). There is a widespread opinion that some peoples (in particular, the Kazakhs and Turkmens) did not allot lands to fixed groups of herders and that the pasture was used by the first to arrive with his herds. This opinion demands qualification. In the first place each major tribe or group of tribes had its region of habitation, well known to its neighbors, within which its migrations took place. And when we read, for example, that among the Altaic Telengit in the early nineteenth century "there was no strict order in the choice of places to migrate and in the length of time spent in them" (Tokarev, 1936:12), we must keep in mind that the Telengit (like other Altaic groups) occupied a strictly fixed territory. Consequently, there was free movement but only within designated boundaries. It would have been difficult to maintain peace and order otherwise. Of course the herders frequently used pastures belonging to others, but only with the agreement of the proprietors. Secondly, even on their own territory, a group's migration was hedged by various constraints. Usually all groups agreed on the routes of migration. Who was migrating where in the steppes was well known. It was judicious not to encroach on pastures to which a strong and rich clan had laid claim. The stable ties of the herder to the pastures he had made his own is clearly shown by the example of

the Turkmens, who dug wells in the desert to water their livestock and then claimed the wells as their own. It was natural that as owners of a well, they also used nearby pastures, although the land was considered the property of an entire tribe (a group of clans). Theoretically any kinsman or even an outsider could drive his animals onto that land, but how could he water his livestock if well water was often barely sufficient for its owners?

The character of the temporary associations (and therefore joint settlements) among the nomads depended also on assuring forage for their livestock. Among many peoples (for example, the Kirghiz) winter settlements were the most numerous; these as a rule remained in one place all winter. It is no accident that in Uzbek and some other languages the ancient Turkic word meaning "wintering place" (*kishlak*) was used for a settlement or "village." In Mongolia, however, the most dense settlements were around rivers and lakes in the summertime: "At the wintering places the population dispersed, and each yurt [dwelling] was placed at some distance from the next" (Markov, 1976:106). Among the southwestern Turkmens as well, larger settlements sprang up in summer. Nomadic groups usually returned to the same summer place, and their stay there was the longest of the year—from three to six months.

The established habits of migration

could change rapidly when war or the threat of war forced the herders to leave their usual dwelling places. The necessity of closing ranks during a period of military danger could force the nomads to live together in large temporary settlements, even though this was very inconvenient for pasturing livestock. For instance, in the twelfth and thirteenth centuries Mongol settlements often numbered in the thousands of inhabitants. The political situation could also have a significant influence on the character of the economy. In the eighteenth and first half of the nineteenth century when there were frequent wars and raids, the Kirghiz preferred to raise horses—the most mobile form of livestock. After the Kirghiz were annexed to Russia in the last half of the nineteenth century, under peaceful conditions, sheep-raising became the chief occupation in the Kirghiz economy, and the number of cattle and camels increased as well. Curtailing of pasture and the demands of the market also affected the composition of the herds.

Although extensive livestock husbandry was the foundation of the nomads' economy, they were not averse to other occupations that could supplement this economy. Practically all the nomadic peoples at various stages of their history practiced supplementary agriculture, hunting, trade, and crafts. Throughout the ages the possibility of seizing neighbors' wealth has been a great temptation, and for many nomadic societies, as indeed for sedentary ones, predatory wars became an important supplement to their peacetime economy. Agriculture occupied an ever increasing role for certain groups, and the cycles of agricultural work had to be considered as they organized their migrations with livestock. Their movements then depended not only on the character of the pasture but also on the time for the harvest of their cultivated lands.

Migratory herding was not humankind's most ancient occupation. As archaeological excavations have shown, it was preceded by a complex livestock-raising and agricultural economy with a relatively sedentary way of life; only husbandry had a more pastoral character. The Aryans, who came from the north into India in the second millennium B.C., are an example of a society with this kind of economy. Why then did true nomadism originate just at the beginning of the first millennium B.C.? After all, the population of the Eurasian steppes had had extensive experience with animal husbandry even earlier.

Horses—the most important animal to the steppe nomads—had been domesticated by the third millennium B.C.

There were probably a variety of reasons that induced many peoples to change from a complex economy to a more specialized one. Climatic changes could have been one important reason for the development of herding as an independent way of life. The climate became more arid from the third millennium. Then a short period of increased moisture around the middle of the second millennium once again gave way to a new dry period in 1200–500 B.C. During this time a number of early agricultural civilizations underwent a decline—both on the north shore of the Black Sea (Tripol'e) and in some southern regions of central Asia (Namazga) (Dolukhanov, 1987:37). With the increased aridity of the climate came an increase in the steppe and semidesert territories that could be used effectively only as pasture for livestock. Nomadic animal husbandry thus originated with a change in natural conditions when it proved impossible to retain the earlier mixed economic forms.

Sedentary peoples saw the nomads as barbarians, destroyers of culture. However, the nomadic herders created their own culture, which reflected the demands and possibilities of their way of life. Movable dwellings, clothing suitable for horseback, a wealth of felts and leather utensils—even writers in Classical times noted these accoutrements of the nomadic lifestyle. Nevertheless, some features of the nomadic culture were slow to evolve, and many traditions of the sedentary (or semisedentary) way of life persisted—for example, the production of ceramics and cumbersome metal utensils. The culture of the later nomads (from the first centuries A.D. on) was more adapted to the migratory way of life. While readily accepting many of the achievements of their sedentary neighbors, the nomads made important independent contributions to world culture. They improved equine harness and stimulated the widespread use of trousers and sabers. They introduced some forms of milk product, and popularized hunting with birds of prey. They also invented the bowed string musical instrument.

Nomadic societies were always characterized by a strong social order based upon principles of kinship. The individual was a part of the "clan" (a group of blood relatives), and the clan was a part of more distantly related communities, which in turn constituted the tribe. This

An ancient grave. Tuva, 1970s. Photograph by S. Vainshtein, courtesy of Institute of Ethnography, Moscow and Leningrad.

organization guaranteed a reliable defense against enemies. Behind the solitary group of a few families wandering the steppes stood an invisible, populous army of fellow tribesmen ready to carry their revenge to anyone who injured one of their own. Although livestock was the private property of individual owners, it was marked with a brand (Mongol: *tamga*) common to the entire clan or to an even larger kinship group. Tradition traced the origins of the clan back to a single ancestor and frequently even several tribes were considered kinsmen, since they also shared an ancestor. This belief in a common origin promoted political alliances.

The nomads' lives were regulated by customary law that affirmed certain norms of human association. Over time traditions and customs changed, but at every epoch the steppe peoples recognized martial prowess, hospitality, respect for elders, love for children, and ready aid to kinsmen as virtues. A funeral and wake was considered an important social obligation that ensured the dead person a good life in the next world; harsh retribution awaited those who dared to profane the grave of a kinsman. Friendships between men often developed into sworn brotherhood. The patriarchal character of the society by no means excluded respect for women.

From ancient times the nomadic societies were divided into two major classes, the aristocracy and the common people. Although ancient custom proclaimed communal right to the land, well-off herders often seized the best pastures for their personal use. The aristocracy did not necessarily possess any real power. But the entire political history of the nomads shows the repeated rise of charismatic leaders capable of subordinating their fellow tribesmen, neighboring tribes, and even neighboring peoples. The nomads, accustomed to harsh living conditions and taught from childhood to ride horseback and use weapons, were famed as fine warriors. Because of the strict discipline imposed by the nomadic rulers ("khans"), these warriors became a formidable military force.

The nomads brought frequent calamities to their sedentary neighbors. The Great Wall of China, much of which was built in the third century B.C., serves as a lasting memorial to the terror the nomadic hordes inspired. However, relations between the nomadic and settled worlds extended far beyond warfare. Steppe and oasis were always connected by a mutually profitable trade. In exchange for livestock, leather, and wool, the herders received grain and handicraft products. In some cases agricultural districts were simply part of the nomadic world: Herodotus, for example, writing in the fifth century B.C., speaks of Scythian cultivators. The nomadic steppes of Transoxiana—between the Amudar'ya and the Syrdar'ya—are an example of another sort: here a large stock-raising district was included in the economy of the oases (Karmysheva, 1980). Nomadic and sedentary peoples sometimes formed political alliances. From the eleventh to thirteenth centuries, Russian princes involved the steppe peoples in their internecine wars, using the armed might of the nomads one against the other. Political alliances were cemented by ties of marriage. For example, the mother of the renowned Russian prince and military leader Aleksandr Nevskii was a Polovtsian girl, and in 1223 the Russians and Polovtsians fought together against a Mongol army.

It is even more difficult to distinguish between nomadic and sedentary peoples in the history of central Asia. The kingdoms that originated in the oases often extended their power over their nomadic neighbors. Whenever the nomads themselves conquered agricultural districts, they settled in the oases in large numbers, took up a sedentary or semisedentary lifestyle, and intermingled with the local population. From earliest recorded times, wherever conditions permitted, the nomads led a semisedentary life. This was true of the majority of Turkmens, Karakalpaks, Uzbek-Aralians, and the Kazakhs living in the Syrdar'yan basin (Zhdanko, 1961:58). Some members of a Turkmenian family would migrate with livestock while the others grew crops.

The processes that led some nomads to take up a sedentary way of life had already begun in the Scythian era and did not cease throughout later times. Usually, it was impoverished nomads with a small number of livestock who settled down. But the reasons for this process are more complex. It is often written that the nomads could not exist without economic ties to sedentary peoples. This is a controversial conclusion. Perhaps they could, but history has never made the experiment, since the nomads have never lived in isolation. From earliest times the advantages of sedentary settlements as administrative, trade, and, chiefly, craft centers were clear to the nomads. Therefore the nomad environment included its own cities even in ancient times. For the most part these cities had been founded by a sedentary population and had later fallen into the possession of a nomad state (for example, the medieval cities on the banks of the Syrdar'ya (Tolstov, 1947)). But in some cases the nomads themselves founded new cities, where craftsmen from as far away as China and France

were brought together to work. Such cities originated, for example, during Chingis-khan's empire. It was the nomadic elite that needed these cities, and as soon as the administrative system maintained by military power weakened, the cities were abandoned.

The last flowering of the nomadic way of life was in the Middle Ages when powerful nomadic kingdoms—in particular, that of Chingis-khan—arose. More recent times brought a decline in nomadism. By the end of the seventeenth century the Manchu rulers of the agrarian state of China had established their dominion over the nomad state of Mongolia. In 1731 considerable numbers of Kazakhs voluntarily accepted Russian hegemony. In central Asia the nomads were weakened by the constant predatory wars that the feudal kingdoms carried on among themselves. The nomads lost control of the large territories they needed for extensive herding. For instance, the annexation of the Crimea to Russia in 1783 put a virtual end to nomadism in the south Russian steppes. By the eighteenth and nineteenth centuries the sedentary peoples of Europe and Asia had far outdistanced the nomadic peoples in cultural development and had begun to excel in military power. Nomadism came to represent a historical anachronism both as economic system and way of life. Therefore, when there was a famine among the Kazakhs in the early nineteenth century, the tsarist administration furnished foodstuffs and then insistently recommended measures for a rapid adaptation of the nomads to settled life.

In the nineteenth and early twentieth centuries nomadism was still practiced by large groups of peoples of the Russian empire: Kazakhs, Kirghiz, Turkmens, Buryats, Tuvinians, Kalmyks, Altaians, Khakass, Yakuts, and some Uzbeks, Azerbaijani, Nogaians, and Bashkirs. But by this time nomadism was not so much an economic system based on extensive mobile animal husbandry. Instead, it had become a cultural identity, stoutly maintained even among semi-nomadic and semisedentary peoples who had abandoned truly nomadic forms of animal husbandry.

In Russia archaeological investigation of the ancient nomadic cultures began in the eighteenth century. It originated with the famous gold artifacts from the Scythian era that were sent to Peter the Great from Siberia in response to his decree of 1718 ordering the collection of ancient and remarkable things ("everything that is very old and unusual") for the Peterburg Museum (Kunstkamer). Excavation of Scythian kurgans on Ukrainian territory in the nineteenth century also brought important materials to light. However, archaeological work reached massive proportions only after the revolution.

Unique monuments like the Pazyryk, Noin-Ula, Arzhan, and Issyk kurgans, as well as Gaimanova and Tolstaya Mogilas, were explored in Soviet times. The creation of academies of science in the national republics of Central Asia and Kazakhstan and of scientific research institutes in the autonomous republics of south Siberia promoted the development of archaeology. Now there are large groups of experienced archaeologists in every republic who participate actively in intellectual life. It is not mere chance that the Soviet-French symposium on the problems of nomadism was held in Alma-Ata in 1987. The data from archaeological excavations are reflected in numerous publications, and the objects found continually enrich the collections of museums located in all regional centers as well as in the capitals of republics. Archaeological work in recent decades has permitted us to investigate the physical monuments of the origins of nomadism, to recognize new traits in the complex and rich culture of the nomads, and to reach an understanding of the continuous historical connection between the populations of steppe and oasis.

The accumulation of ethnographic data about the peoples of Russia became a recognized scientific goal in the eighteenth century also. In 1776–1780 the first synthetic ethnographic work, I. G. Georgi's *Beschreibung aller Nationen des Russischen Reichs, ihrer Lebensart, Religion, Gebräuche, Wohnungen, Kleidungen und übrigen Merkwürdigkeiten* (Bds. 1–4, St. Peters-

burg; in Russian, 3 vols. 1776–1777), described the nomadic and seminomadic peoples. In the nineteenth century studies continued to be published, and the second half of the century was characterized by Russian society's growing interest in ethnography. For example, by the early twentieth century a wealth of ethnographic publications on the Kazakhs had accumulated (Masanov, 1966).

Ethnographic investigations reached a fully professional level in the Soviet period. Groups of ethnographers, including many representatives of the studied nationalities, were established in the academies of science of all the republics. Ethnographic observations led to deeper investigation of the more or less complex economies of the nomads and permitted us to distinguish the separate large category of seminomadic peoples. Traditional social organization—in particular, the extended family-tribal structure—and material and spiritual culture were studied. A large group of authors summarized the data, with due regard for the changes taking place after the Soviet revolution, in the collections *Narody Srednei Azii i Kazakhstana* (The Peoples of Soviet Central Asia and Kazakhstan, 2 vols. 1962, 1963) and *Narody Sibiri* (Peoples of Siberia, 1956). *Istoriko-etnogaficheskii atlas Sibiri* (Historic-Ethnographic Atlas of Siberia: *Atlas*, 1961) was the first summation of a painstaking comparative investigation of the culture of the peoples of the region. Work has begun on a historic-ethnographic atlas of Central Asia and Kazakhstan, and the result can already be seen in a series of publications. Soviet ethnographers continue to pay close attention to transformations in the lives of the peoples of the country, including those who were once nomads.

The Culture of Eurasian Peoples, Prehistoric Times Through the Middle Ages

TOP
Earring. Gold, turquoise. Issyk kurgan, southeast Kazakhstan, fifth or fourth century B.C., Sakas. 3.1 centimeters long. IIAE MA 37/49. Kazakh Institute of History, Archaeology, and Ethnography, Alma-Ata.

BOTTOM
Funnel-shaped earrings. Gold, soldered ring. Besoba burial, near Aktyubinsk, northwest Kazakhstan, sixth or fifth century B.C., Sauromatae. 6.8 centimeters long. IIAE MA 10/6a, b. Kazakh Institute of History, Archaeology, and Ethnography, Alma-Ata.

OPPOSITE, TOP
Cat frontlet plaque. Piece from a bridle. Gold. Tasmola V, northeast Kazakhstan, seventh or sixth century B.C., Sakas. 4.3 by 3 centimeters. IIAE MA 115. Kazakh Institute of History, Archaeology, and Ethnography, Alma-Ata.

BOTTOM
Horse and rider plaque. Gold. Tenlik kurgan, Taldy-Kurgan region, southeast Kazakhstan, third or second century B.C., Sakas. 4.3 by 3.9 centimeters. IIAE MA 135a, b. Kazakh Institute of History, Archaeology, and Ethnography, Alma-Ata.

PAGE 9
Earring. Gold. Mynshukur burial, Taldy-Kurgan region, southeast Kazakhstan, twelfth to tenth centuries B.C., early nomads. 4.2 centimeters in diameter. IIAE MA 31/1 SAE-80. Kazakh Institute of History, Archaeology, and Ethnography, Alma-Ata.

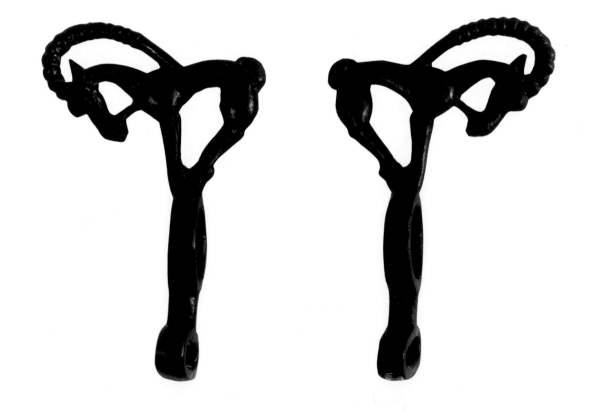

Carved buckle. Griffin head with depictions of a boar and goats. Horn. Tasmola, northeast Kazakhstan, seventh or sixth century B.C., Sakas. 5 by 4 centimeters. IIAE MA 736. Kazakh Institute of History, Archaeology, and Ethnography, Alma-Ata.

Ram buckle from a garment. Bronze. Nagornensk burial, Aktyubinsk region, northwest Kazakhstan, sixth or fifth century B.C., early nomads. 7.6 by 3.4 centimeters. IIAE MA NG-1. Kazakh Institute of History, Archaeology, and Ethnography, Alma-Ata.

Sculptured goat finials. Pieces from a harness. Bronze. Tasmola, northeast Kazakhstan, seventh or sixth century B.C., Sakas. 11.2 centimeters high. IIAE MA 677a, b. Kazakh Institute of History, Archaeology, and Ethnography, Alma-Ata.

Three-legged kettle. Bronze. Alma-Ata, south Kazakhstan, fifth or fourth century B.C., Sakas. 38 centimeters in diameter. IIAE MA 1007. Kazakh Institute of History, Archaeology, and Ethnography, Alma-Ata.

TOP

Inkwell. Kashin, underglazed. Sarai Berke (Sarai al-Dzhedid), fourteenth century, Mongols. 5.9 centimeters high. GE Sar 263. Hermitage, Leningrad.

BOTTOM

Girth buckles. Bronze. Nagornensk burial, Aktyubinsk region, northwest Kazakhstan, sixth to fourth century B.C., early nomads. 6.7 by 6.8 centimeters. IIAE MA NG 2/1, 2. Kazakh Institute of History, Archaeology, and Ethnography, Alma-Ata.

OPPOSITE

Apothecary jar. Fired clay with graffito. Sarai Berke (Sarai al-Dzhedid) or the Crimea, fourteenth century, Mongols. 23.8 centimeters high. GE Sar 296. Hermitage, Leningrad.

TOP

Belt. Leather, silver, stone. Eighteenth century, Mongols. 92 centimeters long. GE Ts-1777. Hermitage, Leningrad.

BOTTOM LEFT

Deer lock. Bronze. Site of find unknown, fourteenth century, Mongols. 5 by 4.5 centimeters. GE Op.Sh 1452. Hermitage, Leningrad.

CENTER

Horse-shaped lock with key. Bronze. Sarai Berke, fourteenth century, Mongols. 4 by 4.6 centimeters. GE Sar 922a, b. Hermitage, Leningrad.

RIGHT

Bracelet. Gold. City of Bulgar, fourteenth century, Mongols. 5.5 to 6 centimeters in diameter. GE 30 704. Hermitage, Leningrad.

The Scythians and Sakians, Eighth to Third Centuries B.C.

Larisa R. Pavlinskaya

The earliest period in the history of Eurasian nomads is called "Scytho-Sakian" from the names of the two major groups of tribes, the Scythians and the Sakas. During this time cultures developed throughout the Eurasian steppes that so resembled each other in general form and specific features that they might be assumed to be a single culture. These likenesses can be seen in the weapons, in the harnesses of the riding horses, and in the art—especially in the peculiarities of its representational style, which has been labeled "Scytho-Siberian wild-animal style." General traits characteristic of the cultures of the Eurasian steppes of the first millennium B.C. are also evident in the religious beliefs, burial customs, forms of social organization, and much else. None of the following periods of the history of Eurasian nomads were anywhere near as uniform as that early period when cultural unity predominated over ethnic and local differences.

The Iranian language (or, more accurately, various dialects with some degree of closeness to Old Iranian, i.e., Avestan) was probably spoken at that time throughout the entire band of the Eurasian steppes, although the inhabitants represented a variety of anthropological types. Caucasoid tribes lived in east Europe, Turkestan (Soviet Central Asia), and south Siberia, while the Mongoloid type predominated in the population of central Asia.

The written texts of Ancient Greece, Assyria, Babylon, and China—early states with which the nomads were in constant contact—are valuable sources of information about the culture of the ancient nomads. In these accounts, which are not completely detailed, we find descriptions of the nomadic economy, daily life, customs, and beliefs, as well as the names of individual tribes and the narratives of historical events.

According to the Greek historian Herodotus (5th c. B.C.), the Scythians inhabited the steppes north of the Black Sea between the Danube and the Don (the territory was therefore called Scythia), the Sauromatae lived farther east in the Volga basin and the southern Urals, and the Maeotians dwelt in the steppes of the northern Caucasus. Massagetae and Sakas populated Turkestan and Kazakhstan. The Greeks knew very little about the tribes who lived north of the Scythians and east of the Sakas. They were told that the northern regions were inhabited by the

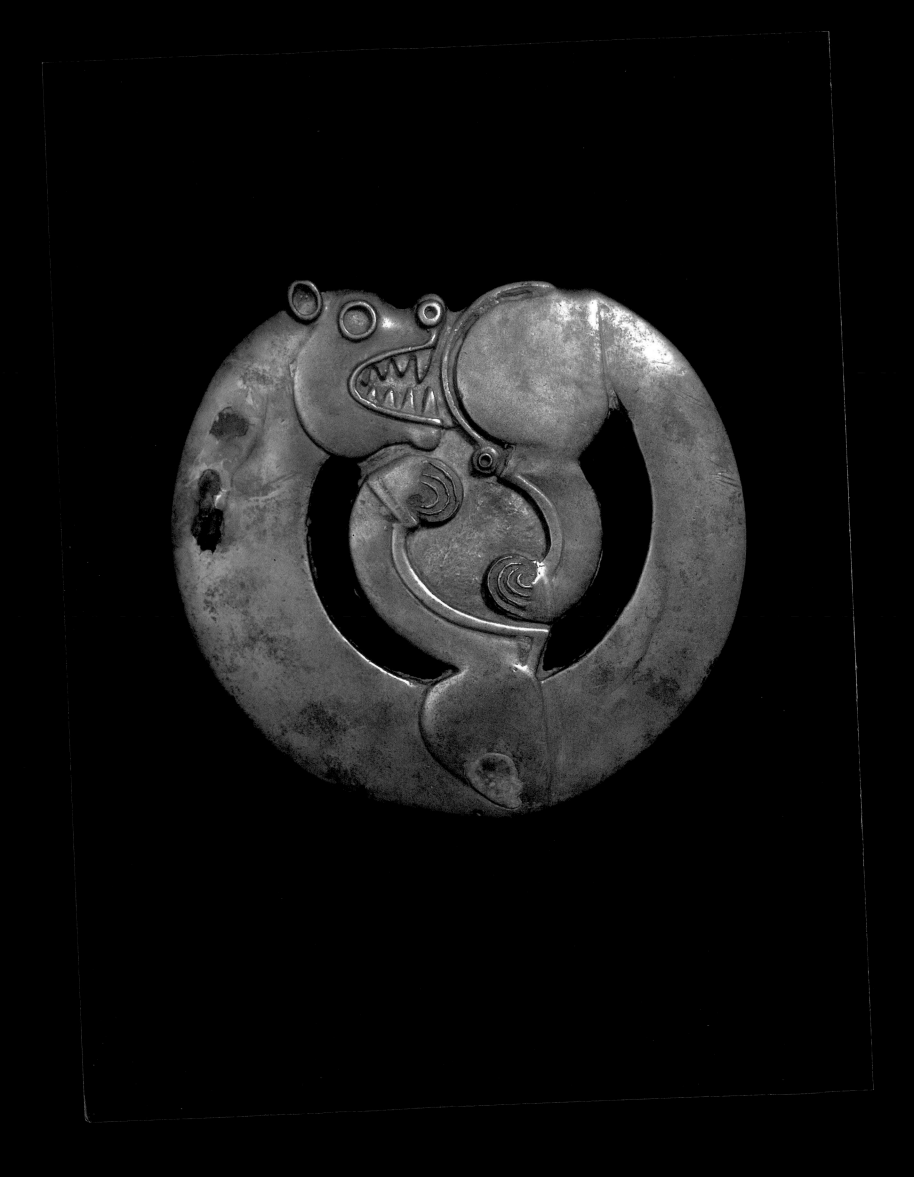

PAGE 18
Ceremonial lamp. Copper. Alma-Ata, fourth to second century B.C., early nomads. 30 centimeters in diameter. IIAE MA AA-1. Kazakh Institute of History, Archaeology, and Ethnography, Alma-Ata.

The lamp is from a set of items found in a distinctive steppe "fire temple" excavation in 1979–1980. The sanctuary consisted of a round clay platform (150 square meters) on which were the remains of a large open hearth and numerous bones of domestic animals. Bronze kettles and sacrificial altars, as well as lamps, are usually found in such sanctuaries.

This lamp and the figures on it have a mythological significance connected with the fire cult. The rider carrying a bow is evidently the personification of the Indo-Iranian sun god, Mithra. The Avesta and Rgveda speak of him as the "master of cattle" and "possessor of broad pastures." Perhaps it is to these attributes that the procession of zebu along the rim of the top refers. Mithra lived on the summit of the World Mountain, evidently symbolized here by the lamp's conical base. Other figures on the lamp, unfortunately, were not preserved.

OPPOSITE
Coiled panther plaque. Bronze. Arzhan kurgan, Tuva, south Siberia, eighth century B.C., early nomads. 25 centimeters in diameter. TRM K2-20. State Museum of the Tuva A.S.S.R., Kyzyl.

This plaque, a breast ornament from a horse's harness, is one of the earliest known works of Scythian art and a magnificent example of a shape determined by the object's intended use.

TOP
Kettle with conical base. Bronze. Alma-Ata district, south Kazakhstan, sixth to fourth century B.C., Sakas. 39 centimeters in diameter. IIAE MA 1008. Kazakh Institute of History, Archaeology, and Ethnography, Alma-Ata.

This kettle was never used, and its maker did not even polish it. It was probably hastily made especially for the burial of a Sakian aristocrat.

BOTTOM
Ceramic pot from the tomb of the Golden Man. Issyk kurgan, southeast Kazakhstan, fifth to fourth century B.C., Sakas. 18 centimeters high. IIAE 37/10. Kazakh Institute of History, Archaeology, and Ethnography, Alma-Ata.

Early Eurasian nomadic tribes. Eighth to third centuries B.C.

fabled Hyperboreans, the one-eyed Arimaspians, and gold-guarding griffins.

Extensive animal husbandry—the basic occupation of the Scythians and Sakians—determined their mobile way of life. To assure forage for the animals they raised (horses, sheep, cattle, and, in the Asian steppes, camels), they were forced to move from one pasture to another. Their chief type of dwelling was a wagon covered with felt (these wagons are known from clay models found by archaeologists). Women and children rode in the wagons during migrations; the men spent most of their lives in the saddle, pasturing and protecting their herds. The mobility of the nomadic societies made great migrations possible; powerful waves of nomads rolled far beyond the boundaries of the Eurasian steppes.

One such migration was the resettlement of the Scythians in the late eighth century B.C. from Turkestan and Kazakhstan to the steppes bordering the Black Sea. This movement, which roiled the steppes, was the beginning of the nomads' invasion of the kingdoms of southwest Asia and Asia Minor. According to Assyrian sources, the Scythians (the "aš-ku-za" or "iš-ku-za") appeared in southwest Asia around 670 B.C. and played an active role in the military politics of such kingdoms as Assyria, Urartu, Media, Mana, and others (D'yakonov, 1956:224ff.). Entering into shifting alliances with one or another of

these kingdoms, Scythian detachments took part in martial raids, destroying and pillaging the opponents' cities. At the end of the seventh century the Scythians became the overlords of Urartu and Mana. But the growing strength of these alien nomadic tribes worried their allies, and in 594 the Median king invited all the Scythian commanders to a feast and then killed them. Deprived of military leadership, the Scythians returned to the northern shores of the Black Sea.

In the mid-sixth century B.C. the most powerful state of the time, Persia, went to war against the nomads. The first military actions against the Sakas and Massagetae ended in a defeat for Persia. The Persian army had marched into Massagetae territory, and having tricked the queen's son and his warriors by leaving a decoy camp for them to capture, fell upon this portion of the Massagetae army as it celebrated and destroyed it, capturing the prince. When the Persian king, Cyrus II, refused to bargain, the Massagetae queen attacked in fury with all her forces and destroyed the Persians almost totally. Cyrus II perished in the battle (Herodotus 1.211-14, 1987). The Persians were partially successful in subduing the Sakas and annexing their territory only during the reign of Darius I (522–486 B.C.; Struve, 1968:58).

Darius's military campaigns against the Scythians on the Black Sea were less successful. In 513, to avenge himself for past depredations in

Top, Left

Early nomads' weapons. Dagger. Copper. Near Minusinsk, south Siberia, fifth century B.C., Tagar culture. 28.9 centimeters long, MAE 1298-32. Knife. Bronze. Altai, south Siberia, seventh century B.C. 16 centimeters long, MAE 2406-1. Peter the Great's Museum of Anthropology and Ethnography, Leningrad.

In the Scythian era the hilts of knives and daggers were often decorated with depictions of birds and beasts of prey; the image of the griffin, which the Scythians borrowed from Asia Minor, was popular in south Siberia. The ancient nomads may have believed that the characteristics of these birds and animals were transmitted through magic to the warrior and his weapon.

Top, Right:

Vase. Silver. Chertomlyk kurgan, fourth century B.C., 70 centimeters high, GE DN 1863-1/66. Hermitage, Leningrad. This vase was crafted in the Greek style but with Scythian motifs.

Bottom

Scythian horseman. Sketch by M. V. Gorelik.

The Golden Man. In 1969–1970 archaeologists from the Kazakh Academy of Sciences found the so-called Golden Man during excavations at the Issyk burial site, 45 large kurgans located not far from Alma-Ata. The remains of the corpse and the grave goods, buried in the fifth or fourth century B.C., were preserved in full.

The burial chamber (right) was 2.9 by 1.5 meters and built out of dressed fir logs. There were various dishes in the south and west sections of the chamber, and the north part contained the remains of the body lying directly on the wood floor.

The large number of gold articles that had decorated the body were preserved in their original position, making it possible for Soviet Archaeologist K. A. Akishev to reconstruct the costume in which a young nobleman had been sent off to the next world. The end result of the reconstruction (left), which took three years to complete, is a unique model of the ceremonial dress of a Sakian aristocrat; it is 215 centimeters tall and is in the collections of the Kazakh Institute of History, Archaeology, and Ethnography, Alma-Ata (IIAE MA 9).

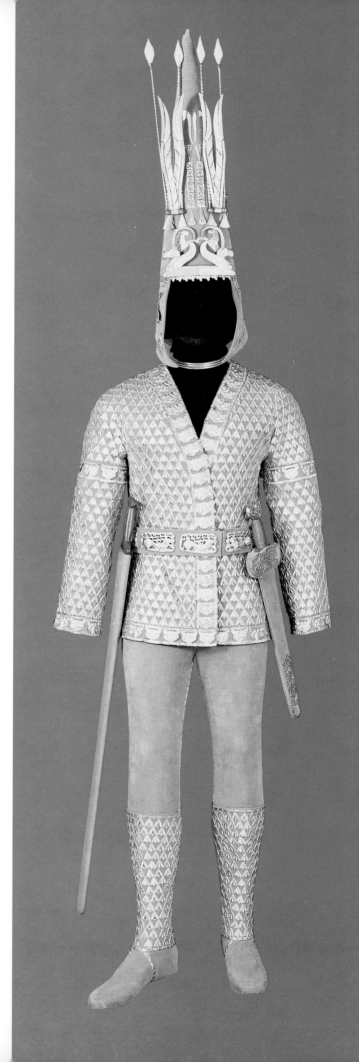

PAGES 24-25
Golden Man's headdress ornament. Gold, wood. Issyk kurgan, southeast Kazakhstan, fifth to fourth century B.C. Sakas. 17.5 by 10 centimeters. IIAE 37/98. Kazakh Institute of History, Archaeology, and Ethnography, Alma-Ata.

southwest Asia, he invaded their lands. The Scythians resorted to tactics similar to those that the Massagetae had used against Cyrus II. Dividing into three detachments, they began to retreat, blocking up wells and springs on their path, destroying vegetation, and attacking individual detachments of Persians. The Scythian ruler Idanthyrsus sent a message to Darius: "We have neither cities nor sown land among us for which we might fear—that they be captured or destroyed—and so might be quicker to join in battle against you to save them" (Herodotus 4.127, 1987:326). The Persians lost a good part of their army and had to leave Scythia. In the fourth century B.C. the Scythians, Sakas, and Massagetae were forced to defend themselves against attack by Macedonian troops commanded by Philip II and then by his son, the famous military leader Alexander of Macedon.

But warfare was not the only form of relationship between the steppe nomads and the peoples of southwest Asia and central Europe. Diffuse trade and cultural contacts also united these two dissimilar worlds. From the sixth century B.C. the Scythians were strongly influenced by Greek culture, and their history from that time on is closely connected with Greek city-colonies on the north shore of the Black Sea, such as Olbia, Panticapaeum, and Chersonesus, which were founded to further the flourishing Mediterranean trade in which the Greeks played a leading role. They furnished the Scythians with wine, olive oil, and the products of their workshops. These products, which were much in demand among the Scythian aristocracy, included gold and silver ornaments manufactured by Greek craftsmen specially for the northern nomads. Carpets from southwest Asia and ceramics and silk from China also found their way into the northern steppes.

To obtain such goods, the nomads participated actively as intermediaries in the trade. Caravan routes pierced the steppes in all directions. By way of the nomads, bronze mirrors passed from Olbia to the Volga, beyond the Don, and into the foothills of the Ural mountains; ornaments of Greek work made their way to the Caucasus, and vases from Achaemenid Iran reached the Ural foothills. The steppes served as an expansive trade route between east and west, north and south. The nomads exported domesticated animals and hides, and their wars enabled them to satisfy the demand in many kingdoms of the ancient world for "living wares"—i.e., slaves (Grakov, 1971:52).

Incessant wars and constant resistance to the pressures of the powerful states of southwest Asia and central Europe led the steppe nomads to put their societies on a permanent military footing, and their commanders reached new heights of power and wealth. They used their military positions to claim inherited privileges and developed dynastic states. The royal power took on an ideological basis: it was ascribed to a divine origin.

In the fourth century B.C. the Scythian king Ateas created the first nomadic state in history by uniting all the nomadic and settled tribes of the Black Sea steppes under his rule. This kingdom lasted until the first century B.C. when a new wave of nomadic tribes, the Sarmatians, poured out of Asia, engulfing the steppes of east Europe. Rulers also headed tribal confederations of Sakas and Massagetae, and sometimes royal power fell into the hands of women, who headed armies just as male rulers when there was a military threat (Herodotus 1.205, 1987).

The royal power relied on the support of the aristocracy, the elders and representatives of individual clans, tribal leaders, and the military elite that rose out of successful campaigns. The exalted social position of the rulers, the representatives of the royal family, and the most distinguished and wealthy section of the nomads' society is confirmed by archaeological monuments, which offer material evidence to supplement the information from written sources.

Golden Man's headdress decorations.
Gold, goldleaf, wood. Issyk kurgan, southeast Kazakhstan, fifth to fourth century B.C., Sakas. Horse plaques, 6.5 by 4.8 centimeters each, IIAE MA 37, 38. One of a pair of snow leopards with mountain peaks, IIAE MA 37/66, 67. Argali, or wild sheep, 1.6 centimeters high, IIAE MA 37/97. Arrowlike ornament with plates shaped like bird wings, 38 by 4 centimeters, IIAE MA 37/99, 100. Bird on tree, 13.9 by 14.2 centimeters, IIAE MA 56, 59. Kazakh Institute of History, Archaeology, and Ethnography, Alma-Ata.

The Golden Man's headdress is rich in symbolism. Decorations representing winged animals, mountains, birds in trees, and arrows pointing upward are obvious symbols of the heavens. Their concentration on the upper part of the garments is an ancient and widely practiced tradition; the placement of spirit images on the upper or lower parts of ceremonial costumes of nineteenth and twentieth century Siberian shamans corresponded to the spirits' positions in the upper and lower cosmic spheres.

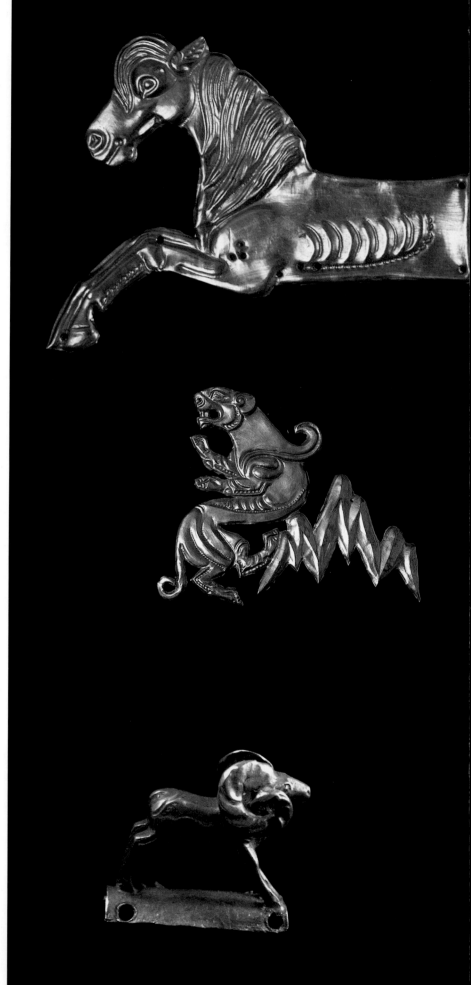

Saddle cover applique. Leather. First Pazyryk kurgan, Altai, fifth century B.C. 34 centimeters long. GE 1295/250. Hermitage, Leningrad.

OPPOSITE
Plaque. Gold. West Siberia or Altai, fifth or fourth century B.C. Si 1727 1/6. Siberian Collection of Peter the Great.

These ornaments are examples of the Scythian wild-animal style in representational art.

A characteristic feature of the landscape of the steppes is the *kurgan*, the earth and stone hill erected over ancient graves, the largest of which are 20 meters high and 60 meters wide. These are the graves of the rulers of large tribal confederations and the nomadic aristocracy. The best-known kurgans on the Black Sea steppes are Kul'-Oba, Solokha, Pyat' brat'ev, Tolstaya Mogila, and Chertomlyk; in Kazakhstan, Issyk; in the Altai, Pazyryk, Bashadar, and Tuekta; and in Tuva, Arzhan.

Unfortunately, the majority were pillaged in ancient times, but those spared are stunning in the wealth of gold and the general splendor of the burial inventory. For instance, at Tolstaya Mogila the graves of a young queen and a child—evidently, her son—remained undisturbed. The woman's entire costume once gleamed with gold: large gold plates were fastened to her headdress, and all her clothing, including her footwear, was sewn with little gold plaques or platelets. The woman's neck was jeweled with a massive gold torque weighing 478 grams and depicting seven little lions creeping up on a young deer. On her temples she wore large gold pendants depicting a goddess; there were massive gold bracelets on her wrists, and her fingers were covered with rings. The child's grave was no less rich; his skeleton was lavishly strewn with the gold platelets that had once decorated his clothing. The central burial chamber, that of the ruler, had been pillaged, but outside it archaeologists found a sword in a gold-covered scabbard with scenes showing animals in combat and a massive gold pectoral—a beautiful example of the ancient art that made the kurgan world famous.

Herodotus described the funeral of a Scythian king as a gloomy but magnificent event. The king's corpse was mummified, lifted onto a chariot, and carried around to the subject tribes, whose representatives joined the cortege. The procession ended in the sacred land of the ancestors, where a grave had been prepared. Along with the king, the Scythians buried one of his concubines and several servants and horses, who were all to serve him in the next world.

Archaeological finds confirm many details of this description. Mummified corpses of rulers in the Pazyryk kurgans of the Altai had concubines buried with them. The remains of servants were found, and horses lay outside the burial chambers. A carriage and many varied items were lowered into the grave. The largest number of horses was found in a kurgan in the northern Caucasus; 360 horses lay around tethering-posts specially erected in the grave pit, and another 50 were found in the mound above it.

Common people were buried differently. The kurgans of ordinary nomads rise barely a meter above the ground. Simple swords (bronze or more rarely iron), lance points, and arrows

were laid beside the buried man. Sometimes a bit was placed there as a symbolic representation of his steed. The contrast between the royal vaults and the graves of common people is evidence of the great differentiation in property and social status typical of the Eurasian nomadic peoples in the first millennium B.C.

The burial of a nomad man was always that of a warrior who fought on horseback. His main weapons were a small bow, javelins, heavy spears, battle axes, and short swords (*akinakes*; 30 to 50 centimeters). Along with light cavalry, the nomads had heavily armed mounted detachments of *cataphractarii* as the army's main striking force. These warriors were clad in bronze helmets and armor made of small copper and iron plates sewn on leather and were additionally armed with long iron swords. But such expensive equipment has been found only in the larger kurgans, which suggests that the aristocracy made up the heavy cavalry. It is thought that the cataphractarii first arose among the Sakas and Massagetae and that the concept was then borrowed, first by the Persians and later by Alexander of Macedon (Tolstov, 1948: 212).

The nomads considered war and pillage an honorable, and therefore constant, occupation. "When a Scythian kills his first man, he drinks his blood; of all those he kills in battle he carries the heads to the king. When he has brought in a head, he takes a share of whatever loot they have obtained, but without bringing a head he has none" (Herodotus 4.64, 1987:303). The Scythians used the scalps of slain enemies to decorate the bridles of their steeds; numerous scalps testified to the valor of the warrior. "Once a year each governor, each in his own district, brews a bowl of wine from which the Scythians drink who have killed their enemies. If they have killed none such, they may not drink of the wine but sit aside, dishonored. This is indeed the greatest disgrace among them" (Herodotus 4.66, 1987:304). The Scythians made wine cups from the skulls of their fiercest enemies. The martial character of the ancient nomads' society created the basis for the cult of a god of war. His shrines were established on a high platform built up on bundles of brushwood, and a short sword symbolizing the god was set up there. Not only animals but people as well were sacrificed to this god. "Of such of their enemies as they take alive they sacrifice one out of every hundred....They pour wine on the men's heads and cut their throats into a bucket. This they then carry up on to the pile of firewood and pour the blood on the sword" (Herodotus 4.62, 1987:303).

Scythian mythology, as outlined in general terms by Herodotus, shows a complex ideology, in which the understanding of nature and society characteristic of ancient man is reflected in an original way. We know the chief gods of the

Golden Man's costume decorations. Gold. Issyk kurgan, southeast Kazakhstan, fifth to fourth century B.C., Sakas. Two of thirteen deer's head plaque-overlays for belt strap, 4.1 by 3.1 centimeters each, IIAE MA 37/41–53. Plaque-overlays of deer with twisted torso, 8.8 by 4.8 centimeters, IIAE MA 37/43, 44. Horse and elk decorations for dagger sheath, 15.7 by 4.1 and 13.4 by 5.5 centimeters, respectively, IIAE MA 37/47, 48. Kazakh Institute of History, Archaeology, and Ethnography, Alma-Ata.

Altogether more than 4,000 gold objects, most of them costume ornaments, were found in the Golden Man's grave. A profusion of decorative gold plaques of various types were sewn to his garments. Those on his belt depicted stylized deer, a popular motif in Scythian and Sakian art. The horse and elk that decorated his dagger sheath have twisted torsos, a characteristic of the early nomadic wild-animal style that conveys disquiet, impulsiveness, and tension.

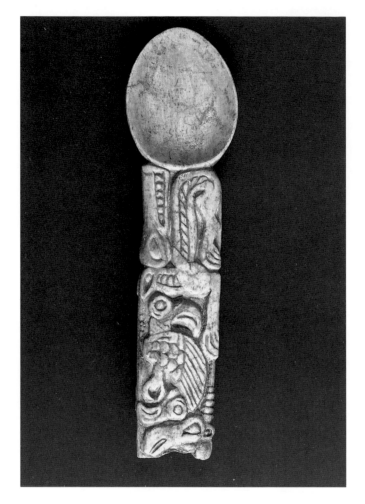

Scythian pantheon. The most revered of them was the goddess Tabiti, whom Herodotus identified with the Greek Hestia (Herodotus 4.59, 1987). The concept of clan community and the unity of all the Scythian tribes is embodied in the image of this goddess, and she is connected with the royal house and the royal hearth (Artamonov, 1961:58). Therefore, the highest oath was that to the "royal Hestias" [goddess of the hearth]. It is probably Tabiti who is depicted sitting on a throne in a high headdress.

The other chief god was Papaeus, the sovereign and progenitor of the Scythians; Herodotus identifies him with Zeus. In the hierarchy of Scythian gods, just below Tabiti, Herodotus names Papaeus and his wife, Api, the earth goddess. Papaeus is the god of the sky and the sun; his marriage to Api evidently symbolizes the union of sky and earth, which gives life to the world.

The sun god was chief in the pantheon of the Saka-Massagetic tribes. "Of the gods they worship the sun only," Herodotus informs us, "to whom they sacrifice horses,...to the swiftest of all gods they assign the swiftest of all mortal things" (Herodotus 1.216, 1987:130). The ritual complex of Ulug-Khorum, uncovered by archaeologists in Tuva, bears witness to the great significance of the sun cult among the nomads: A colossal depiction of a wheel—an ancient symbol of the sun—was laid out in stones on the ground there (Grach, 1980:62–65).

Archaeological work in recent decades has substantially enriched our knowledge of the life of the early nomads. Every year archaeologists discover monuments that give us insights into new and different facets of the culture of the Scytho-Sakian world. For a long time the ancient Eurasian nomads were thought to have had no writing system. But in 1969–1970 during excavations of the Sakian kurgan Issyk (5th–4th cc. B.C.), near Alma-Ata, a silver cup was found bearing an inscription in an as yet unidentified script. Writing was evidently still in a rudimentary stage among the nomads at that time, but its very existence testifies to a high level of culture in the nomadic society of the first millennium B.C. (Akishev, 1978:59).

The most remarkable archaeological find relating to the ancient nomads is the set of kurgans at Pazyryk in the Altai excavated by S. I. Rudenko. They were pillaged in ancient times, but the permafrost that formed when they were exposed to the air preserved objects that under

ordinary conditions would have rotted in the earth. Archaeologists brought a large collection of cloth, felt, wood, and leather artifacts out of the graves. Among them were Persian pile carpets and delicate Chinese silks. The finds at Pazyryk offer us visible evidence of one stage of the ancient nomads' burial ceremony and many of their other customs, as well as unique information about their art. We even know the process they used to decorate their bodies with tattoos.

The original character of the early nomads' indigenous art attracts the attention of everyone who comes in contact with it. Although humans were occasionally depicted, the Scytho-Sakian representational art is dominated by animal images connected with a symbolic system that we have yet to fully decipher. The Scytho-Siberian wild-animal style is distinguished by its kinetic character, motion marked by a high degree of tension. Deers jump at a "flying gallop," predators tear at horse or antelope, and animals with twisted hindquarters, hindlegs pointing upward, are a recurring element. This style creates a sensation of force and dynamism. There is a saturation of images and an expressive plasticity about the wild-animal style: in many cases the form of one animal is covered with smaller figures of animals and incised lines that further emphasize the basic shape.

Sacrificial altar. Stone. Chance find, Kuraili area, Aktyubinsk region, northwest Kazakhstan, sixth or fifth century B.C., early nomads. 29.5 centimeters in diameter. IIAE MA 10/3. Kazakh Institute of History, Archaeology, and Ethnography, Alma-Ata.

Archaeologists have found more than sixty stone sacrificial altars used by the Sauromatian tribes of the lower Volga and the region south of the Urals. The altars are three- or four-legged; the feet are most often shaped like wolves' heads with eyes, ears, and gaping jaws emphasized. The altars are found in the graves of women, probably priestesses.

OPPOSITE TOP
Bone spoon with carved handle. Zhalgyz-oba burial, Aktyubinsk region, northwest Kazakhstan, sixth or fifth century B.C., early nomads. 12 by 2.4 centimeters, IIAE MA AAO-74/53. Kazakh Institute of History, Archaeology, and Ethnography, Alma-Ata.

The carving on the spoon handle is an example of the characteristic maximal use of space in the Scythian wild-animal style.

BOTTOM
Quiver hook. Bronze. Syntas burial, Aktyubinsk region, west Kazakhstan, sixth or fifth century B.C., Sauromatae. 7 by 5 centimeters. IIAE MA S-11/51. Kazakh Institute of History, Archaeology, and Ethnography, Alma-Ata.

The curved part of the hook is shaped like an eagle's head with a powerful beak and big eyes in sharp relief. The upper half shows a wolf's head with nostrils, fangs, large eyes, and ears emphasized. The object reflects the qualities needed by a warrior or hunter—strength, sharp sight, and a keen sense of hearing and smell.

Golden Man's jewelry. Gold. Issyk kurgan, southeast Kazakhstan, fifth or fourth century B.C., Sakas. Torque, 13 centimeters in diameter, IIAE MA 37/46. Ring, 2.5 centimeters in diameter, IIAE MA 37/50. Kazakh Institute of History, Archaeology, and Ethnography, Alma-Ata.

A torque worn around the neck was typical of Scythian and Sakian dress. As a rule these were made from a single piece of gold and evidently were never removed from the wearer's neck, but the Golden Man's torque came apart and could be taken off. The custom of wearing a massive neck hoop did not disappear with the Scythians and Sakians: in the early twentieth century Yakut women still wore such ornaments.

The Golden Man's ring depicts a god-king—possibly Mithra, the Sakian sun god—with a radiant crown.

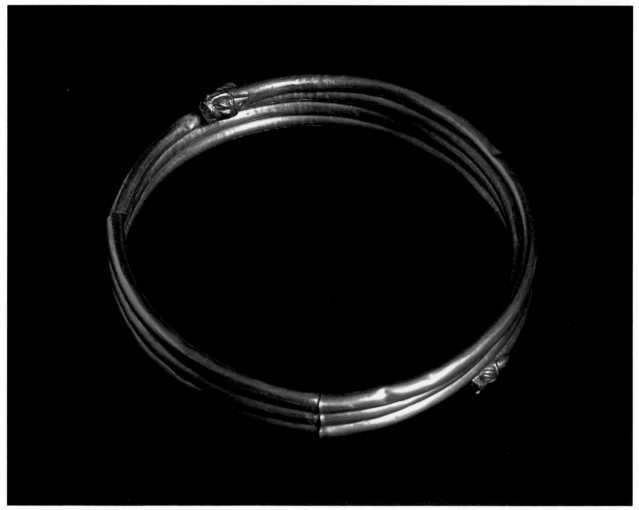

The sources of the art of the early nomads can be traced to the representational traditions of the population of the Eurasian steppes during the Bronze Age in the second millennium B.C. At an early stage of development (8th–6th cc. B.C.) the wild-animal style had a limited subject matter, static composition, and a degree of conventionality that indicated its continuity with the art of the preceding period. But the Scythians' years in southwest Asia influenced their art. Southwest Asian motifs, combined with the animal images characteristic of the nomads, can be easily distinguished in early examples of Scythian art. This influence is most apparent in the representational traditions of the Sakas and the tribes of the Altai; images of lions, griffins, and winged animals, undoubtedly adapted from the southwest Asian cultures, were widely distributed (Akishev, 1978:25; Artamonov, 1973:219–226; Rudenko, 1953:86).

A series of traits appeared early in Scythian and Sakian art that permit us to distinguish in it an independent set of images. New subjects (panthers and griffins) became popular, new compositional devices arose (wild beasts coiled in a ring, paired images), and a new plasticity—a rhythmic alternation of mass and line—developed. The wild-animal style flourished from the sixth to fourth centuries B.C. Traits that were only hinted at in the early stages became predominant and determined the unique

character of the art. Images of predators, fantastic animals, and fighting animals were widely distributed. Decorative elements and artistic generalization were naturally combined with realism. Researchers are unanimous in accepting the wild-animal style as a manifestation of the outlook of the nomads in that tumultuous epoch when life consisted of migrations, raids, and wars.

The images and subjects of this unique art reflect the mythology and beliefs of the ancient nomads. The animal figures are connected with their concepts of the structure of the universe and mythological space and time, but it is difficult to say "whether we see in these memorial depictions of gods transformed into animals symbols of these gods or personifications of cosmic forces" (Raevskii, 1977:173).

The art of the early nomads reflects their widespread cultural ties as well. Considering it a crime and humiliation to accept foreign customs, the Scythians and Sakas nevertheless did not disdain other people's art and willingly made use of ornaments and dishware brought from other lands. The Scythians of the Black Sea coast accepted the representational norms of the Greeks. The many gold and silver objects manufactured by Greek craftsmen for the Scythians represent a fusion of classic and barbarian traditions. The items had to reflect the world of images already familiar to the nomads, and animals and scenes from Scythian mythology predominate. But the overall artistic formulation is in the spirit of Greek art.

Before the excavations of the Pazyryk kurgans, it was chiefly Scythian and Sakian metal artifacts that came into the hands of scholars. These objects were usually made by the nomads themselves. By the first millennium B.C. the nomads knew how to cast bronze, work iron, and temper steel, and they were excellent jewelry makers as well. In the finds at Pazyryk the nomads' favorite animals were depicted in the same style in wood, felt, leather, and bone and in decorations of dwellings, clothing, steeds, weapons, and all sorts of utensils.

Art was an integral part of the nomads' daily life. Closely connected with mythology and religion, it kept them in touch with the world of the gods and the times of legendary ancestors.

With the era of the ancient nomads, a new and colorful page—one vital to understanding the further path taken by the development of nomadic cultures—began in the history of the peoples of the great belt of the Eurasian steppes.

TOP LEFT

Ram. Bronze. Krasnoyarsk region, south Siberia. Seventh or sixth century B.C., Tagar culture. 5.3 centimeters high. MAE 252-17. Peter the Great's Museum of Anthropology and Ethnography, Leningrad.

TOP RIGHT

Coiled beast harness plaque. Bronze. Anan'ino burial, Kama River banks, near Elabuga, west of the Urals, Anan'ino culture, seventh to third century B.C. 7.7 centimeters in diameter. MAE 1093-85. Peter the Great's Museum of Anthropology and Ethnography, Leningrad.

BOTTOM LEFT

Goat head finials. Bronze. Kzyl-Tagan treasure, Taldy-Kurgan region, southeast Kazakhstan, seventh or sixth century B.C., early nomads. 11.3 and 11.5 centimeters high. IIAE MA YaV-23/1, 2. Kazakh Institute of History, Archaeology, and Ethnography, Alma-Ata.

BOTTOM RIGHT

Saddle-girth plaque. Bronze. Besoba burial, Aktyubinsk region, northwest Kazakhstan, sixth to fourth century B.C., Sauromatae. 6.2 by 6.9 centimeters. IIAE MA

TsKAE-76/1. Kazakh Institute of History, Archaelogy, and Ethnography, Alma-Ata.

The normally placid camel is shown here in a threatening pose with bared fangs that are more typical of beasts of prey; the figure displays all the aggressiveness and power of the reproductive instinct. The Iranic tribes of the Scytho-Sakian world, including the Sarmatians, worshipped the camel; the fact that the Turkic peoples made the word for camel a part of their proper names is a much later reflection of this early cult. Iranian mythology treats the subject of a battle between two bull camels: the Avesta tells us that "their camels—fierce, sharp-humped, and lustful—rear and fight fiercely with each other." The motif of the camel may reflect an archaic new-year fertility ritual.

OPPOSITE

Kettle. Bronze, mountain goat handles. Krasnoyarsk region, south Siberia, Tagar culture, seventh or sixth century B.C. 29 centimeters high. MAE 3909-7. Peter the Great's Museum of Anthropology and Ethnography, Leningrad.

The Huns,
Third Century B.C.
to Sixth Century A.D.

Evgenii I. Lubo-Lesnichenko

A new period in the history of the nomadic animal herders of Eurasia began in the late centuries of the first millennium B.C.: political dominion was transferred from the Scythians and Sakas to other peoples. The Sarmatians became the rulers of the steppes north of the Black Sea, and the Huns took over the Asiatic part of the nomadic world.

Classical writers applied the name Sarmatian to the confederation of tribes who drove the weakened Scythians off the steppes between the third and first centuries B.C. This confederation was formed from tribes of Sauromatae, the closely related Dacho-Massagetae, and a number of other groups. They settled on the broad plains around the Volga and the southern foothills of the Urals, and in the fourth to third centuries B.C. they began moving into the northern Caucasus and Scythia. The movement of the Sarmatian tribes westward was part of a general migrational process that rolled across the steppes in a broad wave at the end of the first millennium B.C. and the beginning of the Christian era; it has been called "the great resettlement of peoples" (Smirnov, 1984:114).

The Sarmatian invasion of Scythia was accompanied by brutal military clashes. One historian of the first century B.C. reported that the Sarmatians "ravaged a large part of Scythia and destroying utterly all whom they subdued they turned most of the land into a desert" (Diodorus of Sicily 2.43, 1935:29). The Scythian

domain had contracted sharply in the third and second centuries B.C.; the Scythians retained only lands on the delta of the Dnepr and the steppes of the Crimea, where their new capital, Scythian Naples (Neapolis), arose. By the first century B.C. the Scythians had lost all of the steppelands north of the Black Sea, and Roman authors began to apply the name of Sarmatia to what had been Scythia (Rostovtsev, 1925:43–44). From classical sources we know the names of the largest Sarmatian tribes or confederations: the Aorsi (between the Don and the Caspian), the Rhoxolani (between the Don and the Dnepr), and the Iazyges (between the Dnepr and the Danube) (Pliny the Elder, 1947:IV.12.80).

The political union of the Sarmatian tribes gave impetus to the dissemination of some traits of their culture. In culture the Sarmatians belonged to the Scytho-Sakian world, but their traditions had a number of distinctive features that make it easy for the archaeologist to distinguish Sarmatian relics. For example, as military science underwent further development during the Sarmatian era, long swords and plated armor

Hunnic central Asia. 135 B.C. After Gumilev, 1960.

Hun warrior. Sketch by M. V. Gorelik

OPPOSITE
Skull. Dzhety-asar, south Kazakhstan, first to third century A.D., local nomadic population. IE KhAE-81. Institute of Ethnography, Moscow and Leningrad.

In the Hunnic period artificially elongated skulls were fashionable; they must have been produced by binding childrens' heads while the bones were still soft to create the desired shape.

PAGE 40
Embroidered material. Silk. Noin-Ula, north Mongolia, first century A.D., Huns. 19 by 10 centimeters. GE MR 2521. Hermitage, Leningrad.

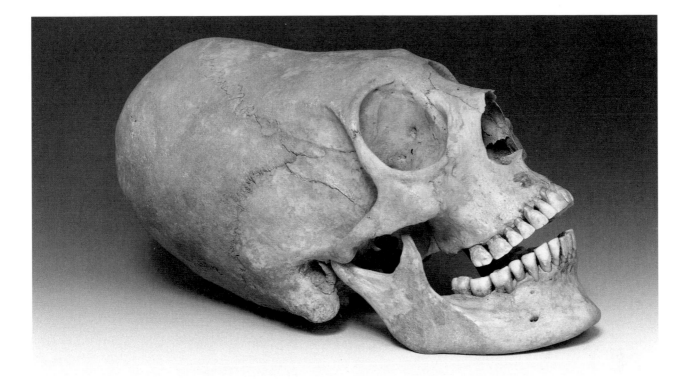

came into wide use, and heavily armored horsemen became even more important. The Sarmatians evidently also brought with them religious beliefs unknown to other peoples of the Scytho-Sakian environment. Their concepts of life beyond the grave are reflected in certain features of their burials: the body was positioned in the grave on a diagonal with the head to the south, chalk was sprinkled on the bottom of the grave, and pieces of it were placed beside the body. These customs, which have not yet been convincingly explained, were peculiar to the Sarmatians.

In the visual arts, the wild-animal style continued, but composition became more static as ornament became more elaborate. Depiction of human beings was a part of the tradition, and "landscape elements" appeared for the first time: on Sarmatian plaques illustrating mythological or epic subjects, we often see human figures against a background of trees. Predators of the cat family came to be depicted with bearlike limbs and outline. Jewelry ornaments were still usually gold but began to be encrusted with semiprecious stones, especially turquoise; this suggests changes in the esthetic views of the steppe population of Eurasia in the period. Notwithstanding all the innovative elements, the Sarmatian domination overall did not lead to any major stylistic transformations of the culture. The expansion of the Huns left much greater traces on the cultural traditions of the nomads.

The creation of the Hunnic state was a major event in the central Asian political arena in the last centuries B.C. Formed during the rule of the *shan-yü* (mounted commander) T'ou-man, who died in 209 B.C., the empire of the Huns strengthened and spread under his son and successor Mo-tun (208–175 B.C.). In the reign of Mo-tun the Huns (who were called Hsiung-nu in Chinese sources) were at the zenith of their might and occupied a huge territory from Lake Baikal on the north to the Ordos plateau on the south and the Liao River on the east. At the beginning of the second century B.C. the Huns defeated the *Yüeh-chih*, who inhabited the territories of modern west China, and subjugated the population of the oases of east Turkestan. Information about this has been preserved in a letter written by Mo-tun in 176 B.C. to the Han emperor Wen (179–157 B.C.): "I have punished the Wise King of the Right [a Hun official] by sending him west to search out the Yüeh-chih people and attack them. Through the aid of Heaven, the excellence of his fighting men, and the strength of his horses, he has succeeded in wiping out the Yüeh-chih, slaughtering or forcing to submission every member of the tribe. In addition he has conquered the Lou-lan [of the Lop-Nor region], Wu-sun, and Hu-chieh tribes, as well as the twenty-six states nearby, so that

TOP
Fragment of Chinese fabric. Noin-Ula, north Mongolia, first century A.D., Huns. One of four pieces, GE MR 1127, MR 1255, MR 1838, MR 1859. Hermitage, Leningrad.

Chinese silk fabrics found in Hunnic graves are clear evidence that the nomads had no desire to live in isolation from their sedentary neighbors and did not do so. On the contrary, they saw settled peoples as a source of riches. Nomadic aristocrats were pleased to have the luxury goods that came to the steppes through bloody warfare as well as peaceful trade.

BOTTOM
Pendants worn at the temples. Gold, stone. Aktas I burial, Alma-Ata district, south Kazakhstan, third century A.D., Sarmatians. 5.7 centimeters long, IIAE MA 131, 132. Kazakh Institute of History, Archaeology, and Ethnography, Alma-Ata.

OPPOSITE
Kettle model. Ceramic. Kokel', Tuva, south Siberia, first century A.D., Huns. 16.7 centimeters in diameter. MAE KE 40. Peter the Great's Museum of Anthropology and Ethnography, Leningrad.

Models such as this one found in burials prove that kettles had the same shapes in Hunnic times as in the previous Scythian period. Modern kettles with rounded bottoms, which were placed over the fire on hoop-shaped, footed trivets, appeared later.

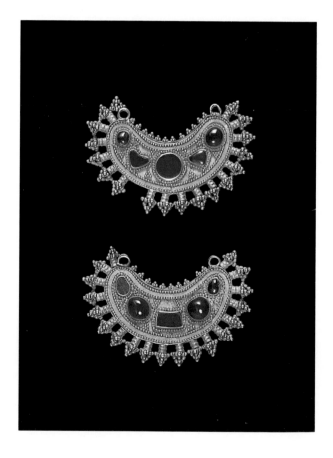

Votive flags. Cloth. Noin-Ula, north Mongolia, first century A.D., Huns. 73 by 17 and 45 by 11.5 centimeters. GE MR 970, MR 2084. Hermitage, Leningrad.

Opposite Left
Parts of arrows. Wood, iron. Kokel', Tuva, south Siberia, first century A.D., Huns. 11.5 and 7.8 centimeters long. MAE KE 19a, b. Peter the Great's Museum of Anthropology and Ethnography, Leningrad.

Right
Model of keg. Wood. Kokel', Tuva, south Siberia, first century A.D., Huns. 11 by 5 centimeters. MAE 68. Peter the Great's Museum of Anthropology and Ethnography, Leningrad.

The models of kegs, kettles, a sword, arrows, and other objects that archaeologists have found in Hunnic burials show substantive evolution in the nomads' concept of life beyond the grave. The Scytho-Sakian peoples usually put real objects into the grave to furnish the dead with the things they needed in the next world. But in the Hunnic era there was a widespread conviction that the deceased could make do with miniatures of the requisite objects. These changes were evidently connected with the appearance of a more refined concept of the soul: perhaps the models were a way of furnishing the deceased's soul with the "souls" of the various objects.

all of them have become a part of the Hsiung-nu nation" (Ssu-ma Ch'ien, 1961:2.168). Under shan-yü Chih-Chih (55–34 B.C.) the political influence of the Huns reached as far as the lower Volga and the Ural foothills and as is recorded in the dynastic history of the western Han, Chih-chih demanded tribute from Ferghana and the states north of it (Pan Ku, 1935:70).

The expansion of the Huns westward significantly increased their trade and other contacts with the western world. The route leading from the west through the northern oases of east Turkestan to the Huns' headquarters in north Mongolia and then southward to north China became active. The artistic products of the Hellenic Near East were delivered to the Hunnic aristocracy along this road, as the famous finds in the graves of Hun rulers in the Noin-Ula mountains (north Mongolia) dating from the first years of the Christian era clearly demonstrate. The eight kurgans excavated in 1924–1925 by an expedition led by P. K. Kozlov contained wool fabrics, tapestries, and embroideries brought to north Mongolia from Sogdiana, Greek Bactria, and Syria. From the Han Empire to the south a huge quantity of various kinds of silk cloth, embroideries, quilted silk, and lacquerware and bronze jewelry came to the Hun headquarters.

Chinese written sources contain much information about this trade and tribute system, which played a significant role in the complex relations between the Hunnic power and the Han empire. The great Chinese historian Ssu-ma Chi'en (2nd c. B.C.) described the Huns as "living in the region of the northern barbarians and wandering from place to place pasturing their animals. The animals they raise consist mainly of horses, cows, and sheep but include such rare beasts as camels, asses, mules, and…wild horses.… They move about in search of water and pasture and have no walled cities or fixed dwellings, nor do they engage in any kind of agriculture. Their lands, however, are divided into regions under the control of various leaders" (Ssu-ma Ch'ien, 1961:2.155).

On the basis of this passage, the Huns were long seen as primitive nomads without agriculture or cities. However, archaeological finds in recent decades and a deeper acquaintance with written sources have given us a better picture of Hunnic society. It has been proved that the basis of the Hun economy was herding, but there were also settled populations, significant diffusion of agriculture, and well-developed production of crafts.

The horse played a leading role in the herders' migrations, hunting, and war. Numerous archaeological finds have given us a good idea of the Hunnic bridles, which had iron or horn cheek-pieces, and pack saddles, which consisted of a wooden framework covered with leather that was often embroidered. Felt

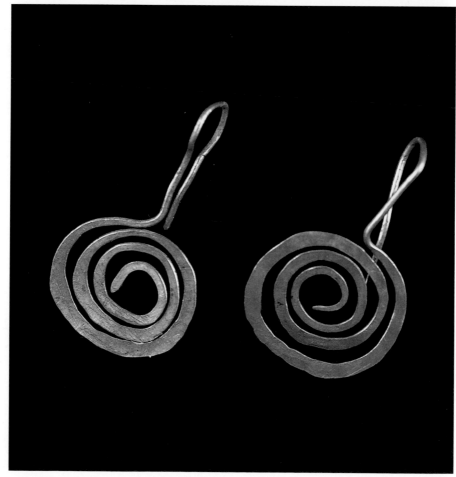

sweatcloths were placed under the pack saddles and a saddle-blanket laid over them (the Huns had no stirrups). Written sources report that in good years one man might have up to nineteen animals to herd, and in difficult times their number could fall as low as four (Egami, 1963:353–354).

War trophies and trade goods were not sufficient to satisfy the varying needs of the population of the colossal Hunnic confederation. The Huns began to develop their own production of agricultural products and crafts. For instance, it is recorded that in the first century B.C. the Huns began developing agriculture on their western frontiers. Now we know that there were a large number of settlements from Hunnic times situated on the territories of Mongolia and

what is now the Buryat Soviet Socialist Republic. Investigation of the Ivolga site (16 kilometers southwest of Ulan-Ude), carried out from 1955 to 1974 by A. V. Davydova, has familiarized us with a previously unknown aspect of Hunnic culture: a settled life, the construction of dwellings and workshops, the cultivation of millet, barley, and wheat, and the production of craft items. Iron and bronze were smelted on the site. Tools, weaponry, household utensils (including a large number of ceramics), and jewelry were found in the town, which was inhabited from the third to first centuries B.C. (Davydova, 1985).

The Huns stemmed basically from the Siberian branch of the Mongoloid race. The well-known Soviet anthropologist M. M. Gerasimov and his students have created sculptural restora-

tions that give us an idea of the physical appearance of the Huns and the populations under their domination. Analysis of the few Hunnic words and proper names that have come down to us seems to confirm the belief that the Huns spoke one of the Turkic languages (Gumilev, 1960:48–49; Maenchen-Helfen, 1973:376–443). However, the question of language is far from resolved, and there are a number of specialists (e.g., Doerfer) who are extremely skeptical of the interpretation of Hunnic words as Turkic on the basis of such sparse data.

The main source of our knowledge of the Huns, Ssu-ma Ch'ien's *Records of the Grand Historian of China*, describes their clothing as follows: "From the chiefs of the tribe on down, everyone eats the meat of the domestic animals and wears clothes of hide or wraps made of felt or fur" (Ssu-ma Ch'ien, 1961:2.155–156). In addition, finds at Noin-Ula suggest that the Hun aristocracy had garments of imported wool and silk fabrics. The Huns wore wide and roomy trousers gathered at the bottom. They also had trousers consisting of two very wide leg pieces that ended in footwear; these were put on separately and fastened at the waist. Felt half-boots, covered with leather and embroidery, were worn on top of them. That the soles of the footwear were also decorated with embroidery is evidence of their habit of sitting cross-legged "Turkish style" (Rudenko, 1962:39–41).

The Huns wore caftans lined with felt and edged with fur. Among the headcoverings discovered at Noin-Ula were two peaked caps of a type *(kolpak)* that was widespread among the nomads of Eurasia. Another type of headgear was a headband with embroidery, ribbons, and earflaps. Women wore flat-topped, cylindrical caps; they plaited their hair in two or three braids, which they covered with a silk sheath decorated with rows of triangular or scalloped pieces of silk (many of these braids were found in the Noin-Ula kurgans). The Huns wore broad belts with decorative bronze buckles. A bronze fibula was fastened to the breast of their garments.

Of the Huns' armament Ssu-ma Chi'en wrote: "For long-range weapons they use bows and arrows, and swords and spears at close range" (Ssu-ma Ch'ien, 1961:2.155). Numerous finds tell us that the Huns had complex bows reinforced with bone or horn overlays. The arrows had iron or bone tips of various types. Finds at Il'movaya pad' (Buryat S.S.R.) confirmed information from written sources about the use of arrows that whistled in flight (Konovalov, 1976:174). Moreover, at the Ivolga site remnants of armor were found, and at Noin-Ula bronze armor and finger-guards. No swords have yet been discovered in Hunnic burials, and our only idea of their appearance comes from wooden models.

Information from excavations casts some light on the Huns' utensils. Like the popu-

Plaque. Silver. Noin-Ula, north Mongolia, first century A.D., Huns. 13.5 centimeters in diameter. GE MR 2970. Hermitage, Leningrad.

Researchers are familiar with Hunnic decorative plates depicting yaks and deer in an artistic style that has nothing in common with Scythian and Sakian art. The Huns apparently worked out their own independent canons of pictorial art, evidenced here in the yak's quiet pose and the elements of landscape in the background.

lation of the Altai in the Pazyryk period (5th–3rd cc. B.C.), the Huns ate at small wooden tables and used wooden, metal, clay, and—probably—leather dishes. Finds of bronze cauldrons with handles and bases should also be mentioned; they were used for cooking meat (Rudenko, 1962:36). Clay utensils ranged in size from small bowls and cups to large vessels one meter high in which grain and food supplies were stored. A large amount of lacquerware made its way from China to the Huns. The year of manufacture—the equivalent of 2 B.C.—scratched on two small lacquer cups found at Noin-Ula served to date those kurgans (Lubo-Lesnichenko, 1969:267–277).

Chinese written sources inform us that the Huns worshipped the sun and the moon and dedicated sacrifices to heaven, earth, and the spirits. There was also a cult of ancestors to whom human beings were sacrificed. We also know that they had soothsayers and shamans. It is possible that a mysterious headband found at Noin-Ula was the paraphernalia of a shaman. The Huns had a profound belief in life beyond the grave and furnished their dead with everything necessary in the world beyond. Animals were sacrificed at the burial. Aristocratic Huns decorated their burial chambers with luxurious carpets and patterned fabrics; gold, jade, and lacquered objects were placed in the graves. The large collection of women's braids in silk sheaths

is noteworthy among the burial inventory. These were probably laid there as a sign of mourning, symbolizing the women's following of their master into the next world. A similar custom was known to many peoples of the world, and in particular to the ancient Greeks: Achilles cut off his curls and put them in Patrocles' hands (*The Iliad*). A number of scalloped silk votive banners was also found in the kurgans (we don't know what role they played in funeral rites).

The burials from Hunnic times offer evidence of a changing conception of the soul and life beyond the grave as the era went on. In the early centuries A.D. the conviction had obviously developed that real objects need not be put into the grave: models were sufficient for the deceased in his new life. For instance, at the burials on the Kokel' site (Tuva, south Siberia), which date from the first to third centuries, it is typical to find models of weapons (a sword, arrows) and utensils (cauldrons, small tables).

Hunnic art was clearly related to the wild-animal style that had taken shape among the early nomads of the Eurasian steppes. The tradition of depicting real or fabulous animals in a frozen pose or in battle continued. The scenes of a yak fighting with a fabulous horned beast and a griffin attacking a deer that decorate a felt rug from Noin-Ula are typical. The animals are depicted according to the fixed convention but with stress on their individual traits. The Huns adapted the traditions of the wild-animal style to their own tastes, using the animals they were familiar with—goats, rams, yaks, horses, camels, elk, and eagles.

The Huns also developed another esthetic style that had nothing in common with the Scytho-Siberian tradition. This representational style is seen on ornamental silver plates found in the burials at Noin-Ula. The yaks and deer on the plates stand in rather clumsy poses, their bodies in profile and their heads facing front. In contrast to the dynamism of the wild-animal style, they are the embodiment of tranquility. Landscape elements, stylized mountains and trees, are introduced on two plates that depict yaks. These are "products of an original character that testify to the formation of an original Hunnic culture" (Artamonov, 1973:121).

The confederation of Hunnic states reached a peak of power in the second century B.C. and from then on was sapped by incessant wars and internal social dislocations. In the middle of the first century A.D. the Hun state divided into northern and southern sections, and the southern Huns fell under the influence of China. In the fourth century B.C. ephemeral Hun dynasties formed repeatedly in the south, but by the fifth century they had all left the political stage and dissolved into the ethnic masses of central Asia and northern China.

The fate of the northern Huns was quite different. After their crushing defeat by the Hsien-pi in 93 A.D., the remnants of the northern Huns moved west, drawing numerous tribes of the Eurasian steppes into their orbit. In the second half of the fourth century they appeared on the southern plains of east Europe. They crushed the Alani and the Goths and created a huge confederation of tribes. In 445 Attila took command and ravaged Gaul and northern Italy.

Reports from European sources characterize Attila as a headstrong and brutal man with a thirst for power who did not stop short at murdering his brother in his drive to consolidate his might. A "lover of war," as the Gothic historian Jordanes (6th c.) called him (Jordanes, 1915:102), Attila was also a politician who knew how to create discord among his enemies. His mobile headquarters resembled a vast city. The wooden walls enclosing the entire population were made of "smooth-shining boards, whose joints so counterfeited solidity that the union of the boards could scarcely be distinguished by close scrutiny.... The courtyard [of Attila's palace] was bounded by so vast a circuit that its very size showed it was the royal palace" (Priscus, as quoted by Jordanes, 1915:101).

Historians inform us of some of the Huns' customs during Attila's time, emphasizing their love for horseback-riding and their facility in archery. "They are beings who are cruel to their children on the very day they are born. For they cut the cheeks of the males with a sword, so that before they receive the nourishment of milk they must learn to endure wounds" (Jordanes, 1915:87). The Huns surrounded their military camps with carts to form a rampart. Despite their martial spirit, they sometimes resorted to divination of the outcome of a battle. Their soothsayers "examined the entrails of cattle and certain streaks in bones that had been scraped" (Jordanes, 1915:106). (The bones referred to were probably scapulae of sheep or other animals that were widely used for divination by the steppe nomads and their neighbors long before Jordanes's observation).

The description of Attila's funeral is most interesting. The king died unexpectedly of overindulgence the night after a feast at which he had taken the newest of a series of very beautiful girls in marriage. When his retainers found him dead the next day, "they plucked out the hair of their heads and made their faces hideous with deep wounds, that the renowned warrior might be mourned, not by effeminate wailings and tears, but by the blood of men." Attila's body was placed in a silk tent "in the midst of a plain.... The best horsemen of the entire tribe of the Huns rode around in circles, after the manner of circus games, in the place to which he had been brought [i.e., the site of the kurgan or burial mound] and told of his deeds in a funeral dirge" (Jordanes, 1915:123–124). The mourners then held a huge feast on top of the kurgan. (Similar customs were observed for a long time among the nomads. Horseback competitions and feasts for large numbers of people still took place at the funerals of wealthy Kazakhs and Kirghiz at the beginning of this century.)

After Attila's death in 453, dissension broke out between the Huns and the peoples they had subjugated. His son, whom the dread conqueror had named to succeed him, was killed in the struggle for power. The Hunnic state rapidly disintegrated, and individual groups of Huns scattered over Europe and Asia. Some settled in Pannonia and Dacia, others in Turkestan and Persia; all of them soon dissolved into the local population.

The Turkic Peoples, Sixth to Twelfth Centuries

Sev'yan I. Vainshtein

Some 1500 years ago the formidable conquerors who called themselves *Türk* (in Chinese sources *T'u-chüeh*) became an important force in the steppes of central Asia. These martial nomadic tribes won a series of decisive victories over their powerful neighbors and in 551 A.D. created what for the times was an enormous state—the Turkic khaganate, which lasted until 744. Chinese historians have posited that the origin of the Turks was connected with the late Huns, but there is no real evidence for this, and the opinions of contemporary researchers about their possible ancestry differ (Klyashtornyi, 1965).

Very little is known about where and how the Turks lived before their rise. Two genealogical legends written from the words of the Turks themselves have been preserved in Chinese annals. These legends evidently have a historical basis. According to the first, the ancestors of the Turks lived on the edge of a large swamp (in other versions, on the shore of the "Western Sea"). Enemies attacked and destroyed them all, except a ten-year-old boy, whom a she-wolf rescued and carried off into the mountains north of the Turfan depression. When the boy grew up, he took the she-wolf to wife. She bore him ten sons, and each of them married a local woman. The most capable of the boys—A-shih-na—became the head of a new tribe that took his name. Soon the number of clans making up the tribe grew to a few hundred. One of A-shih-na's successors led the she-wolf's descendants into the Altai, where they took the name Turk, which, according to the legend, was the local name of the Altai Mountains.

A second legend states that the ancestors of the Turks originated near "So," which some investigators identify with the northern Altai. Until their migration, traditionally dated from 460, the ancestors of the Turks lived farther west. In the Altai they came under the domination of a confederation of nomadic tribes called the Juan-Juan. Information has come down to us that the Turks, among other occupations, mined iron and used it to pay tribute.

In the mid-sixth century a subtle and decisive politician named Bumin took over the Turkic tribes. The Turkic ruler deliberately entered into conflict with the Juan-Juan, sending them a message with an impertinent request for the hand of the khan's daughter in marriage. The khan responded: "You are my ironworker, how dare you make such a proposal to me?" Bumin had the Juan-Juan envoy who brought the answer put to death, and soon afterward (in the winter of 552) went to war against the Juan-Juan and routed them.

Having finished off the Juan-Juan, the Turks moved against their other nomadic neighbors. They subjugated many of the peoples of the Eurasian steppes and seized the north Chinese kingdoms. In the west they conquered central Asia and reached the Volga; in the east their power extended as far as the Yellow River. Individual detachments of Turks repeatedly advanced even farther west and east. By the end of the sixth century, the Turkic khaganate had political, economic, and cultural contacts with the major states of the period—Byzantium, Iran, and China—and struggled against them for control of the trade routes. The "Silk Road," the great caravan route that joined east and west, ended up in the hands of the Turks. Trade during the Turkic khaganate was particularly lively and lucrative, since the Silk Road through the inner regions of Asia became much less dangerous (Gumilev, 1967).

Between the sixth and seventh centuries the Turkic khaganate split into eastern (central Asian) and western (Turkestan) parts. The East Turkic khaganate, weakened by internecine wars, became a protectorate of the Chinese Sui dynasty and from 630–682 was not an independent state.

Nomadic animal herding was the basis of the Turkic economy. As the Chinese annalist noted, "The fate of the *T'u-chüeh* depends utterly and completely on sheep and horses" (Liu Mau-Tsai, 1958:1.333). Some of the population also kept cattle, and oxen were used to haul carts as pack animals, and for ploughing. One of the Chinese annals says that "the horses of the [T'u-chüeh] possess extraordinary endurance and commensurate builds; they can withstand long migrations and are unequaled for hunting" (Liu Mau-Tsai, 1958:1.453).

Horsemen were the formidable and very mobile force of the Turkic armies. That the steed was regarded as the most important attribute of the nomad's life was reflected even in the burial cult. Among the ancient Turkic tribes of the Altai, Tuva, Mongolia, and a number of other regions of Eurasia, a man was buried together with his steed in full harness and saddle. It was in the Turkic environment of the middle of the first millennium that the use of a highly developed rigid saddle with stirrups first became common—all later types of saddle can be traced to the ancient Turkic type. Somewhat later the horsemen learned to wield a saber while riding firmly seated in the saddle (Vainshtein and Kryukov, 1984).

Hunting, in particular the technique of the drive, also played an important role in Turkic economy. The main objects of the hunt in the mountain-steppe regions were mountain goats, deer, and roe-deer (*kosuli*). Cliff drawings of the ancient Turks portray hunting scenes; various

PAGE 54 AND OPPOSITE
Grave monument. Barlyk steppes, Tuva A.S.S.R. ancient Turks. Photographs by L. Potapov (page 54, 1940s) and S. I. Vainshtein (1970s).

Grave monument fragment. Stone. East Turkestan, fifth to seventh century A.D., ancient Turks. 35.5 centimeters high. GE MR 3782. Hermitage, Leningrad.

This head from a grave monument bears a Turkic runic inscription, which unfortunately has not yet been deciphered.

wild beasts are shown. The bow was the main weapon in the hunter's arsenal, but pits and perhaps cross-bows were also used.

To a lesser degree the Turks also practiced agriculture, with millet as their chief crop. Archaeologists have found millet seeds and stone grinders in Turkic graves.

What did the Turks look like? Their appearance combined Caucasoid and Mongoloid traits, but among them were some typical Mongoloids, very similar to the modern Mongols, and others who looked almost entirely European (Vainshtein and Kryukov, 1966). Both men and women wore their hair braided. We have some idea of their clothing from Chinese sources and archaeological finds. They wore long garments made from the skins of domestic and wild animals, including sheepskin, from felt and coarse wool cloth, and from silk they obtained from China. In distinction to the Chinese, the Turks wrapped their robelike garment with the right side over the left (the higher aristocracy, however, tended to imitate the Chinese style). Warriors wore mail-armor and helmets, and some khans even had gold mail. The men's costume always included a narrow leather belt. The aristocracy wore belts with beautiful, lavishly ornamented gold plaques; common warriors had belts decorated with more modest bronze plaques.

Crafts were well developed, in particular, mining, smelting, and forging of iron. Magnificent artifacts made from iron—swords and sabers, lance tips and arrowheads, pieces of harness—have been preserved in Turkic graves. They manufactured decorated metal dishes, including some from silver, and various leather utensils; they were skilled at woodwork and made saddles, frames for yurts, carts, and other artifacts out of wood. Felt-making and weaving were practiced.

The collapsible felt yurt, widespread and possibly even invented in the ancient Turkic environment, was the usual dwelling (Vainshtein, 1976), which many nomadic peoples of the Eurasian steppes borrowed. The Chinese poet Po chü-i (778–846 c.) left a picturesque description of the Turkic yurt, which at that time penetrated even Chinese daily life:

> They gathered wool from a thousand sheep
> And forged two hundred rings for me.
> The round frame from riverbank willows
> Is solid, fresh, easy, and handsome.
> The whirlwind cannot rock the yurt,
> Its breast is hardened by the rain.
> It has neither corners nor nooks,
> But inside it is cozy and warm…
> The felt is a wall against hoar-frost,
> The shroud of snow brings no fear…
> The prince covered his palace with carvings
> What are they beside the sky-blue yurt!

Turkic peoples and their neighbors. Late sixth to early seventh centuries A.D.

One of the major cultural achievements of the ancient Turkic peoples was the development of a writing system. The first published information about Turkic runic inscriptions on stone steles preserved in south Siberia dates from the reign of Peter the Great in the early eighteenth century. Later such runes were found not only in Siberia but in other territories of the Turkic world and in Mongolia, where many Turkic tribes lived in the second half of the first millennium A.D. The writing system, which long remained undeciphered, was called "runic" because of its resemblance in appearance to European runes. It was also called "Orkhono-Enisei" from the place where the first finds were made. The Turkic writing system can be traced back to the Aramaic alphabet, but its closest relation is Sogdian.

Decipherment of the runic inscriptions in 1892 by the Danish professor Vilhelm Thomsen created an important historical source for study of Turkic history (Klyashtornyi, 1964). Most of the inscriptions were epitaphs for military commanders (Malov, 1951). They contain various information about the life of the deceased, including impressive descriptions of the aggressive campaigns of the Turkic khagans. The inscription in verse on the monument to Kül-tegin reads:

In all we went to war twenty-five times,
We gave battle thirteen times,

We took away the realms of those who had realms,
We took away the khagans of those who had khagans,
We forced those who had knees to bend their knees,
We forced those who had heads to bow their heads.

(Stebleva, 1965:114–115)

There are a large number of relics of the ancient Turks' decorative arts. The pictures engraved on objects found in a grave at Kudyrge in the Altai are among the most famous. The horn layer of a certain saddle arch has a dynamic, realistically portrayed hunting scene. The outlines of the drawings are precisely chased. The retention of elements of the Scythian wild-animal style is clear (for example, the depiction of a wounded roe-deer with twisted croup and head turned backward). On the upper part of a boulder from Kudyrge a masculine face with mustache and beard has been incised; below this, three horses and three dismounted riders kneel before a woman and child. The woman wears a headdress with three horns; both she and the child are wearing earrings. Two of the kneeling men, and perhaps the horses as well, wear masks, and one of the men also has on a three-horned headdress (Gavrilova, 1965). The drawing probably depicts a pagan prayer to the ancestral spirits of a deceased woman.

Stele. Kherbisbaar' site, Tuva.

This ninth-century Turkic stele was discovered in 1959 by S. I. Vainshtein; the inscriptions, which were placed on all four sides of the stele, have been translated by A. M. Sherbak. The text shown in the photograph reads:

> For / valorous / men of the people
> I procured three blessings.
> Of life / with my people and my khan, o creator,
> Alas, I did not get my fill.

> (Vasil'ev, 1983)

The little that is known about the religious beliefs of the ancient Turkic peoples comes from the evidence of the Orkhono-Enisei monuments and Chinese annals. They indicate a concept of three worlds—Upper, Middle, and Lower. The highest deity of the Upper World was Tengri (sky), who governed the fates of all living things. The fertility goddess, Umai, and the deities of earth and water (iduq yersub), who inhabited the Middle World, held a special position in the Turk's system of beliefs. The deity of hell, Erlik-khan, ruled the Lower World. A cult of the mountains was known, and the spirits of ancestors were honored. Some investigators think that the ancient Turks practiced shamanism, but there is no incontrovertible evidence for it. One of the runic texts reflects in brief the ancient Turkic legend of the creation of the world: "When the sky above was blue and the earth below was dark, the son of man appeared between them" (Malov, 1951:36; *Religion*, 1987:89).

Even today ancient Turkic stone statues connected with the burial cult can be seen on the Eurasian steppes. The tradition of erecting them probably originated in the Altai sometime between the fifth and sixth centuries and then spread throughout the Turkic tribes. These statues usually depicted a male warrior holding a vessel. The face was carved either in relief or in outline; sometimes both means were combined. The sculptures often showed mustaches, beards,

Silver pot. Seventh or eighth century A.D., ancient Turks. 27 centimeters high. GE BM-1122. Hermitage, Leningrad.

OPPOSITE
Pail with handle. Silver. Seventh or eighth century A.D., ancient Turks. 21 centimeters high. GE SK-620. Hermitage, Leningrad.

hairdress, and earrings, as well as details of clothing, belts, and weapons. The best examples of these stone statues were found in the Turkic aristocracy's rich monuments, in particular, in the memorial to Ton'yuquq near Ulan-Bator and to Kül-tegin and Bilge-khagan in an isolated area on the Orkhon River in Mongolia. (Stone sculptures in varying degrees of skill of execution continued to be put up by the Turkic-language nomads of Tuva, Kazakhstan, Mongolia, and other regions of central Asia as late as the eleventh century (Evtyukhova, 1952; Grach, 1961; Sher, 1966; Vainshtein, 1972; Kubarev, 1984).)

It is impossible to describe Turkic culture as a unity in the ancient era. From the sixth century on, numerous Turkic-speaking peoples settled the vast territory from the frontiers of China and the shores of Lake Baikal in the east to the Danubian steppes in the west. Their political interests and cultural traditions varied considerably. Many of these peoples carried on a bitter struggle against the Altaian (Orkhon) Turks, the T'u-chüeh, who created the khaganate.

In central Asia in the middle of the eighth century, the Uighurs, under the rule of Mo-yen-ch'o, defeated the T'u-chüch decisively and created their own powerful state—the Uighur khaganate (745–840). In Tuva the majestic ruins of Mo-yen-ch'o's fortress and palace have been preserved on an island in the lake Tere-khol', and in the steppes there is a mighty Uighur defensive wall with a system of fortified settlements that crosses Tuva from west to east (the latter was discovered and explored by Soviet archaeologists in the 1950s and 1960s (Vainshtein, 1958, 1964; Istoriya Tuvy, 1964; Istoriya Sibiri, 1968)).

In the mid-ninth century the Uighur khaganate was smashed by Turkic-speaking Enisei Kirghiz who in turn created in the steppes of central Asia a powerful state—the Kirghiz khaganate (Kiselev, 1950; Khudyakov, 1982). Many examples of Kirghiz runic writings can still be found on the Enisei, and their craftsmen manufactured decorated metal and clay utensils, silver and gold ornaments, and weapons; a magnificently decorated gold dish was found in the kurgan of a Kirghiz aristocrat in the Minusinsk basin. The Kirghiz cremated their corpses and buried the remains in huge vaults. They were shamanists, and the ancient Kirghiz word for a shaman, kam, has been preserved among the south Siberian Turkic peoples to the present day.

After the fall of the Uighur khaganate, some of the Uighurs remained in the Tuvan territory and were later diffused among the Tuvinians, but most of them left for other areas of central Asia and Turkestan. They subsequently made one of their most important cultural achievements when at the end of the first millennium A.D. they developed the phonemic

"Uighur" alphabet (written from the top down
and from left to right). Uighurs were the literate
transmitters of written culture in central Asia,
and Sogdian missionaries succeeded in propagat-
ing among the central Asian Uighurs one of the
western religions, Manichaeanism (Bar'told,
1956:1.8–9, 1968).

    A tribe related to the Uighurs, the
Qurykans, were living on the shores of Lake Baikal at the time of the rise of the Kirghiz. They
practiced animal husbandry, breeding handsome
horses, and doing some farming; they also pro-
fessed shamanism. Driven from their homes by
Kirghiz, they moved up the Lena river and
merged with another Turkic people, the Yakuts.
In their *taiga* culture the traditions of the southern steppes (animal herding, dwellings, jewelry,
utensils) and the northern peoples who mixed
with them (clothing, food, etc.) combined into a
new organic whole.

    By the sixth century the main popula-
tion of the Danube basin west of the great belt of
the steppes consisted of migratory Turkic-speaking tribes. They were part of the Avar khaganate,
which lasted until the end of the eighth century.
They were chiefly nomadic hordes, but their
crafts and magnificent decorative arts were
highly developed; the remarkable traditions of
the wild-animal style, which had apparently
already disappeared from the nomadic environment, were used with unexpected power and

Sketch of petroglyph. Kudyrge burial, Altai.

The drawing shows three horses and three dismounted
riders, who are kneeling before a woman and child. The
woman and one of the men wear three-horned headdresses; two of the men and the horses appear to be wearing masks. The vivid drawing probably depicts a pagan
prayer to the ancestral spirits of a deceased woman.
Sketch from Gavrilova, 1965.

OPPOSITE
Facing for saddle arch. Horn. Kudyrge burial, Altai.

Elements of the Scythian wild-animal style (the twisted
croup and turned head of the wounded deer, for example)
are evident in the hunting scene etched on the facing.

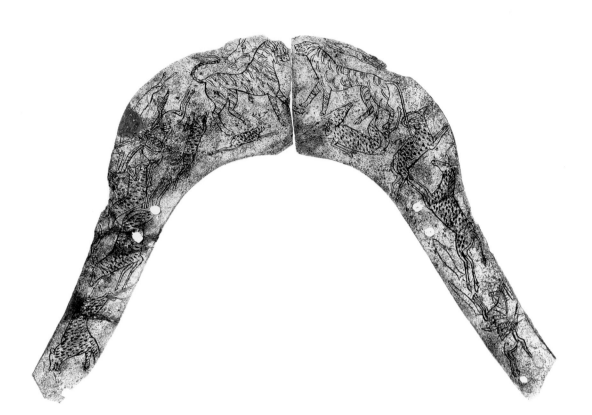

extraordinary expressivity (Laszlo, 1974;
Vainshtein and Korenyako, 1988). The Avars
made frequent raids on Byzantium and the Slavs
before they fell under the blows of the Franks.

As the Hunnic empire disintegrated,
the Turkic-speaking Khazar tribes established
themselves on the steppes near the Caspian Sea
and in the northern Caucasus. From the mid-
seventh century they formed their own
khaganate, which lasted until the tenth century.
By about 750 the khaganate took in a vast territory near the Caspian and Azov seas and a large
part of the Crimea; it bordered on the south Russian steppes. The Khazar capital was the city of
Itil' on the Volga (north of modern Astrakhan;
destroyed in 965 by the Kievan Prince
Svyatoslav). Migrating with their animals, the
Khazars practiced a little agriculture; some of
them settled down. Archaeologists have found
the remains of permanent wooden dwellings that
they used in addition to the collapsible ones of
the nomads. From the eighth century the predominant religion of the Khazars was Judaism;
this is attested both by a letter written by the
Khazar Khagan Iosif (mid-10th c.) and by archaeological finds, in particular, gravestones
depicting the seven-branched candlestick of Jewish ritual that were discovered on the territory of
the khaganate (Taman' peninsula).

The Khazars fought the Arab caliphate
and made raids against the Slavs. The trade
routes from Rus' and other northern lands to
Byzantium went through their capital, Itil'.
Many artifacts from the Khazars' daily life that
testify to their extensive cultural relations
(Chinese mirrors, for instance) were found in
Khazar graves and settlements, especially those
of their last years. The Khazar culture overall has
yet to be fully investigated (Kokovtsev, 1932;
Artamonov, 1962; Pletneva, 1976; Dunlop, 1967;
Pritsak, 1978; Golden, 1980).

The descendants of the T'u-chüeh, who
called themselves the Oghuz, moved west from
central Asia and in the ninth and tenth centuries
settled in the steppes of Turkestan on the lower
reaches of the Syrdar'ya and the Aral Sea. Here
they continued their migratory way of life and
founded settlements that Arab sources describe
as cities. In the first half of the eleventh century a
major part of the Oghuz, under the rule of Seljuk
sultans, conquered Iran, the southern Caucasus,
and almost all of Asia Minor; at the height of
their power they controlled Syria, Iraq, and
Yemen as well. The ancient agricultural population of Azerbaijan and Anatolia took on Turkic
attributes as a result of the Oghuz conquests.
Oghuz tribes who went as far as the boundaries
of the Muslim world and accepted Islam took the
name Turkmens. In 922 Ibn Fadlān, an envoy of
the Caliph of Baghdad, crossed the lands of the
Oghuz in present-day Turkmenia. He wrote that
he saw among the Oghuz "men who owned tens

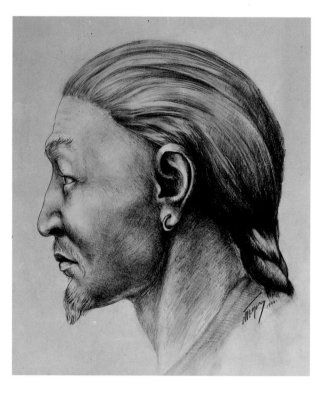

Bronze coins bearing a walking lion and a tribal identifying mark (*tamga:* □ or X) were issued in the Otrar oasis (the mid Syrdar'ya basin), which was the center of the Turkic colony of Kangu Tarban in the early eighth century. Political hegemony there was in the hands of the Kangar (Kengeres), known in later Old Russian and Byzantine sources as the Pechenegs, who roamed the south Russian steppes from the tenth century on. For the Turks, as for many other peoples, the lion was the emblem of supreme authority, and many medieval Turkic rulers bore the name Arslan (Leo).

of thousands of horses and hundreds of thousands of sheep." (Ibn Faḍlān, 1939:33). He described the funeral of a wealthy nomad:

> When one of their [number] dies, they dig a large pit for him in the shape of a house,… they put his short tunic on him, his belt, and his bow…and place in his hand a wooden cup filled with the intoxicating drink (*nabiḍ*), set before him a wooden vessel with…nabiḍ, and bring all his money (māl) and put it in this house with him; afterwards they set him down into it. The house is roofed with planks over him, and something like a clay dome is built over it. Next they take his horses and, depending on their number, kill a hundred or two hundred of them or one and eat the meat, except for the head, hooves, hide, and tail, which they suspend on wooden structures, saying: "These are his horses, which he will ride in paradise." If he had killed men and was a hero, [they] carve wooden images in the number of those he killed, set them up on his grave, and say: "These are his pages, who will serve him in paradise" (Ibn Faḍlān, 1939:27).

It is interesting that until recent times some of the Turkic peoples of Siberia still observed the custom of sacrificing horses at the graves of the deceased.

The oral tradition was well developed among the ancient Turks; they were especially fond of tales of heroes. The medieval epic, "The Book of My Grandfather Korkut," a vivid example of the genre, probably originated in Oghuz tales from the ninth and tenth centuries (Zhirmunskii, 1974:519ff.).

Offshoots of the Oghuz, Turkic-speaking Pecheneg tribes, roamed the south Russian steppes from the eighth to tenth centuries. Ibn Faḍlān described the Pechenegs as "swarthy, strong, and they shave their beards. They are poor, unlike the Oghuz" (Ibn Faḍlān, 1939:27). They repeatedly raided Russian lands. In 1036 the Kievan prince Yaroslav the Wise (978–1054) defeated them decisively.

From the eleventh century the south Russian steppes swarmed with increasing numbers of Turkic-speaking tribes of Kipchaks, whom the Russians knew as Polovtsians. Their economy was based on nomadic animal husbandry, and they practiced some crafts as well. They also fought against the Russian princedoms. Until recently it was still possible to see Polovtsian stone monuments alongside the raised dirt kurgans on the steppes of the Ukraine. In erecting such monuments, the Kipchak were carrying on an ancient Turkic custom that continued in south Russia right up to the thirteenth and fourteenth centuries. But, unlike the ancient Turks, Polovtsians erected statues to women as well as men. Rubruck wrote in the thirteenth century that the Kipchaks "make a great mound over the dead man and set up a statue to him, facing the east and holding a cup in its hand in front of its navel" (Rubruck, 1955:105). The stone statues were objects of veneration by the deceased's relations, and the Polovtsians came to treat them as idols—i.e., the image of the deceased in time gave way to that of a deity (Fedorov-Davydov, 1976:95). The Kipchaks were routed by the Mongol-Tatars in the early thirteenth century, and some of them ended up on the territory of modern Hungary (Golubovskii, 1884; Pletneva, 1958).

In the tenth century Arab geographers were still describing the Turks as a people completely alien to Islam and hostile to Muslims. The basic boundaries between the Turkic tribes and the Islamic peoples also delimited regions where nomadic husbandry and settled agriculture were practiced. Soon after that, however, the situation began to change, and some of the Turkic tribes converted to Islam. It took a few more centuries for Islam to take firm root among the numerous Turkic peoples. Finally only some of the Turkic-speaking peoples of Siberia remained outside Islam.

As Islam became the religion of a number of Turkic peoples in the eleventh and twelfth centuries, new elements were introduced, not only into their spiritual culture but into their way of life and language. At that time the influence of the cultural traditions of the non-Turkic peoples of southwest and central Asia on the nomadic Turks increased considerably. However, the strongest traditions of the pre-Islamic ancient Turkic culture were stubbornly preserved then and much later; this is particularly true of the tradition of oral poetry. Evidence for this is the Kirghiz epos "Manas," which was first written down by W. Radloff in the nineteenth century. The basic stratum of the epic goes back to pre-Islamic times, to the ancient Turkic culture formed long before the influence of Islam made itself felt.

The Mongol-Tatar States of the Thirteenth and Fourteenth Centuries

Mikhail V. Gorelik and Mark G. Kramarovskii

One of the most important events in the history of Asia and eastern Europe was the formation in the thirteenth century of the Mongol-Tatar states ruled by Chingis-khan and his descendants.

The tradition of medieval state systems formed from nomadic tribes goes back to the Ch'i-tan Liao Empire (tenth century). In the twelfth century relatively stable political systems were created by the Mongol-speaking Naiman, Kereyit, and Merkid tribes. The Tatars, widely dispersed along the borders of Tangut and China, were much less united and willingly adapted themselves to the Tangut, Jürchen, and Chinese cultures.

The Mongols proper—a group of tribes from northeast Mongolia who traced their origins from the forests of the Amur basin but had long since become nomads—began moving toward unification around the middle of the twelfth century. But after the death of their khan Qabul, who was seized by the Tatars and turned over to the Jürchen, the unity of the Mongol tribes and clans was destroyed, and a bloody internecine war began.

By the end of the first decade of the thirteenth century, Chingis-khan, a member of an aristocratic family that had fallen into penury, managed through tireless intrigue and military conflict to unite almost all the principal Mongol tribes into a single power. He put his considerable energies into the creation of a militaristic system aimed at constant conquest. Using the traditional nomadic division of troops into units of ten grouped into center, left, and right wings, Chingis-khan greatly strengthened the army by the introduction of well-defined organization, strict discipline, and regular drill. His military-state system turned out to be extraordinarily effective, and his campaigns and those of his grandsons led to the creation of a gigantic empire stretching from the Pacific to the Danube and from Siberia to Burma.

The united empire was short-lived; it reached its farthest boundaries and began to disintegrate by the mid-thirteenth century. However, each of the fragments of the empire became a vast state on its own: the *ulus* (or state of) Jochi (the Golden Horde) seized the lands from the north shores of the Black Sea to Khorezm (Khwarazm) and the Caucasus; the Chaghatai state occupied central Asia, Kazakhstan, and east Turkestan; the empire of Hulegu included Iran, Iraq, and Afghanistan; and the empire of Khubilai (the Yüan Empire) encompassed China, Mongolia, and Tibet.

There are a number of excellent written

Borders of Golden Horde. Thirteenth century.

Mongol warrior. Sketch by M. V. Gorelik.

Idol. Bronze. Site of find unknown, twelfth or thirteenth century. 23.5 centimeters high. GE 30.624. Hermitage, Leningrad.

The exact beliefs represented by this figure are not known, but it testifies to the persistence of pagan beliefs in the early years of the Golden Horde.

Ladle. Gold. Siberia, thirteenth century. 13 centimeters in diameter. GE Sar 1625. Hermitage, Leningrad.

This vessel was among the objects sent in the early eighteenth century to Sankt-Peterburg as part of Peter the Great's famous Siberian Collection. Presumably therefore it was found in Siberia. The bottom of the ladle is decorated with a rosette containing a lotus and an inscription in the "Turkic" literary language and in mirror Arab script (resembling "naskh"). The language of the inscription connects it to the Volga region. The inscription proclaims: "in the year: since the prophet Muhammad went from Mecca to Medina six hundred seventeen [years] have passed." This date corresponds to 617 by the Muslim calendar, or 1220–1221. The ladle's inscription was evidently not original but only copied by the craftsman, and the ladle is 70 or 80 years more recent than the date in the inscription; the motif decorating it is characteristic of the late thirteenth or early fourteenth century.

BOTTOM
Ladle. Silver. West Siberia, second half of thirteenth century. 10.8 centimeters in diameter. GE 53-856. Hermitage, Leningrad.

This silver ladle, with dragon's head handle and benevolent Arabic inscription, comes from a find that included coins from the Golden Horde dated between 1313 and 1362. Vessels like this one and belt ornaments depicting dragons belonged to members of the first-generation officer corps of the Jochid rulers of the Golden Horde.

Case for prayer texts. Silver, gilt. Volga region, fourteenth century. 8 by 7 centimeters. GE V3-108. Hermitage, Leningrad.

Cases for prayer texts made of metal, in this instance gold and silver, were a typical Muslim amulet. However, the decoration on this case is not typical, since Islam forbids the depiction of living creatures. Evidently this prohibition had not yet taken effect by the fourteenth century among the population of the Golden Horde, which had converted to Islam only a short time earlier.

sources that permit us to reconstruct rather accurately and in detail the political, socioeconomic, ethnic, and cultural history of most of these states. These sources include such remarkable works as the Mongolian "Secret History," Rashid al-Din's *History*, accounts of the west European envoys John of Plano Carpini and William of Rubruck, Marco Polo's accounts, the Chinese "History of the Yüan Dynasty," and Russian and Armenian chronicles.

The political system of the Mongol states was based on the interaction of two population groups—the ruling nomads (who were of Mongol and Turkic origin) and the subordinated sedentary peoples. The former made up the military cadres and aristocratic officials; the latter paid taxes and furnished auxiliary military forces. The interaction of these groups took place through an officialdom consisting of educated representatives both of the Mongol-Turkic aristocracy and the conquered peoples. The Mongols widely recruited emigrants from other countries—Tadzhiks, Uighurs, and Europeans in China; Chinese, Uighurs, and Armenians in Iran and Iraq—to work in the bureaucratic apparatus. These newly arrived officials, who had no native links with the peoples they were to govern, were meant to serve as a counterforce to local separatism according to the plan of their Mongol masters. This administrative apparatus was created

to secure a steady flow of material blessings from the subjugated population to the ruling elite. Protection of international trade in luxury goods and keen interest in highly qualified master craftsmen were characteristic of the political and economic life of the Mongolian empire.

The early stages of the empire were not at all conducive to the growth of high culture: the Mongols' unrestrained destruction of innumerable cultural and artistic works in the conquered countries is a well-attested fact. The constructive work that took place in the Mongol-Tatar states and the unique culture that they developed are not as well known. Even those who appreciate the culture tend to attribute its original character only to elements introduced by the sedentary population. But in fact the contribution of the sedentary, and above all the urban, population was only one element of the culture of the Mongol states, although it was often fundamental. What was important was the way in which elements of the urban culture (or, more precisely, cultures) interacted with elements of the nomadic culture. The new cultural entity, although diverse in its sources, was aimed entirely at fulfilling the material needs of the nomadic aristocracy. Wars were conducted and the empire created in order to supply these needs.

Around the middle of the thirteenth century, a feverish activity of rebirth, or more

Paper bill. Thirteenth century, Mongols. 30 by 21.6 centimeters. GE Kh-3027. Hermitage, Leningrad.

This note dating from between 1167 and 1280 passed as currency in the Mongolian Yüan Empire (the *ulus* of Khubilai). It was worth "two bundles" (a bundle was a thousand coins). The inscriptions are in both the Chinese and Mongol languages—the Mongol text is in the oldest *'Phags-pa* script. The circulation of paper currency shows the sophistication of the systems by which the nomads regulated the life of subject countries.

OPPOSITE TOP

Cow's scapula. Inscription in the "Chaghatai" language and Arabic script. Aspara site, Chu River Valley, east Kazakhstan, fourteenth century. IIAE MA AS-1. Kazakh Institute of History, Archaeology, and Ethnography, Alma-Ata.

The inscription in a Turkic language is in black paint on both sides of the bone. Fifteen deceased people are named, among them several who occupied important positions in the city of Aspara and the Chu Valley. The inscription, which takes the form of a litany ("Akh! And Hasan from Kuvaluk we mourn with songs of sorrow. Akh! And Hodjjadj also we mourn with songs of sorrow," etc.), was apparently meant to be read during a funeral rite.

Inscriptions on cows' scapulae were also used for divination, and archaeologists have found one in sixteenth-century layers in Otrar on which is written a list of debtors in a certain part of the city.

BOTTOM

Ewer. Glass. North Caucasus, Belorechensk burial. Italy or Kaffa (Feodosia), Crimea, fourteenth century. 26 centimeters high. GE TB 117. Hermitage, Leningrad.

This translucent green glass ewer is one of the expensive objects imported into the Caucasian steppes, but there are no known analogous objects to help archaeologists date it and determine its provenance. The ribbed body suggests an imitation of silver vessels of eastern or Byzantine origin. Similar objects produced in Europe or the Near East are not rare among the finds that characterize the culture of the Golden Horde and testify to the broad scope of external trade in the period.

exactly, the recreation after decades of wars of an urbanized life, began in the Chingisid states.

No matter how different urban culture was from their way of life, many Mongols, especially the members of the aristocracy, were very well informed of its attractions even before the creation of the Mongol Empire. This familiarity was due to trade, participation in diplomatic missions, and service as mercenaries. In addition, the memory of the city-oriented civilizations of the Liao and Tangut states had been preserved in the steppes of central Asia.

Two approaches to the sedentary population and its culture were developed by the Mongol aristocracy as they conquered and consolidated their empire. Representatives of the first approach believed that conquered settlements and agricultural lands should be destroyed and the entire expanse turned into pasture, and that the population—after pillaging—should be almost without exception exterminated. Representatives of the second school thought, on the contrary, that the sedentary population was a stable source of all sorts of material and spiritual blessings, and for that reason that the growth of cities should be encouraged as centers of crafts, trade, and administrative activity and as places to accumulate and store the wealth the Mongols had amassed.

Yet at the same time the Mongol aristocracy was united in its ideas about the way of life

that suited its new exalted position, down to details of costume, jewelry, hair style, harness, dishware, utensils, and portable dwellings. The manufacture and decoration of these accoutrements of nomad life were the primary, and often the only, task of craftsmen and artists. Foreign trade was carried on primarily to attain these objects. Many crafts and arts specialists were attached to the headquarters of the khans and lesser rulers, creating nomadic cities (ordubasar) with workshops, stores, and marketplaces. Jewelers, armorers, bone- and wood-carvers, makers of wooden furniture, dishware, and leather goods, and women who embroidered and wove rugs worked there.

But palaces and their decoration and the large-scale production of precious dishes, stonework, and ceramics—all of which were in colossal demand—were impossible without the conveniences of city life. This aristocratic demand in turn led to the flourishing of such characteristically urban arts as monumental architecture and painting.

Of course, monumental architecture and its decor, monumental painting, and miniatures in books were not Mongol or even nomadic arts. Yet Mongol consumer taste played a decisive role in the development of cultures in the second half of the thirteenth century and, in particular, the early fourteenth. For instance, in China, under the Mongols, the fashion for white

Bird. Fired clay, turquoise glaze. Sarai
Berke (Sarai al-Dzhedid), fourteenth cen-
tury. 10 by 12.5 centimeters. GE Sar 247.
Hermitage, Leningrad.

OPPOSITE
Seals. Silver. Eighteenth century,
Mongols. Each 10.8 by 10.8 by 8.7 centi-
meters. GE MR 418 and 428. Hermitage,
Leningrad.

The use of large silver seals by important
officials is a tradition that dates from the
period of the Mongol states and was preserved to the early twentieth century.

porcelain with a cobalt design replaced the fashion for celadon. Yüan white porcelain became
instantly popular throughout the empire, and
craftsmen began imitating it in the Middle East
and central Asia. The celadon and cobalt styles
and Chinese ornamental motifs surged into the
West. Similarly old forms of buildings and vessels took on a new appearance influenced by
Mongol fashions.

At the same time, Chinese and Uighur
painting became as popular in the West as
Iranian metalware and ornamental motifs were
in the Far East. A synthesis of Muslim miniatures and Sino-Uighur painting led to the flourishing of Iranian miniatures that was characteristic of the fourteenth through sixteenth
centuries.

Throughout the 250-year period of the
empire, Mongol styles of costume and weaponry
set the mode in dress and jewelry as well as in
offensive and defensive armament in east and
west Eurasia and the fashion for the patterns and
techniques of their decoration. This is the reason

Bowl. Fired clay with graffiti. Solkhat, Crimea. First half of fourteenth century. 35 centimeters maximum diameter. GE Sol 30. Hermitage, Leningrad.

This bowl, typical of those produced in Anatolia (Asia Minor) in the pre-Mongol period, was made in Solkhat (Crimea). In the era of the Mongol-Tatar states, Anatolian traditions were transmitted to the Crimea, to the Golden Horde's city of Sokhat, where a sultan from Asia Minor, Izz-ed-din, lived in the mid-1260s.

The cup bears scenes of a feast in a pomegranate orchard; the young men gathered probably belonged to an *akhi*, one of the brotherhood organizations found in the Crimea and areas around the Sea of Azov in the fourteenth century. The brotherhoods might have originated under Turkish influence or arisen independently in the area; V. A. Gordlevskii traces the origins of the akhi in the area north of the Black Sea to the 1220s.

Associations of young men of the same age, strictly organized and playing an important role in society, were known among all the peoples of Soviet Central Asia; G. P. Snesarev suggests that they originated from the earlier male unions. The young men's gathering took place according to an established ritual and were orgiastic in character.

that the Mongol aristocrat, wearing his "ethnic" costume, hair style, and weaponry, became a hero of graphic arts, for example, in the Persian epos "Shāh-nāme," or the world events in the *History* of Rashid al-Din. This fashion was generally uniform throughout the region from the Amur to the Danube and the Euphrates, and the finest masters of half the world put their skills to work to embody it. Collected and intermingled in the urban centers of the empire, the initially separate and local traditions had, in half a century, arrived at a synthesis that can be called the art of the Mongol empire, and rightfully so, since Mongol tradition played a large role in its creation.

When the unified Mongol empire of Chingis fell apart in the mid-thirteenth century, its successors were four major states. Among them, according to the evidence of Arab authors, only the state of Jochi, the "Golden Horde," the boundaries of which were already formed by the 1240s in the steppe zone between the Irtysh River and the Danube, could be considered a "world power" (Polyak, 1964:29).[1] The Mongols, led by Batu (1227–1254), subdued the Polovtsian or Kipchak steppe and the contiguous agricultural territories of north Khorezm, Volga Bulgaria, the Crimea, and the north Caucasus, whereupon the Kipchak steppe became the center of the new feudal state from 1243. By the mid-

thirteenth century the Polovtsians had evidently lost some of the unique features of their burial rites, including the tradition of erecting stone or wooden statues in specially arranged sanctuaries (Shvetsov, 1979).

The infiltration of the Mongol ethnos into the Kipchak steppe was not great at the time of their invasion. It was the army, not the people, who conquered: the irreversible character of the cultural processes on the territories from the Irtysh to the Danube was due not to the numerical superiority of the Mongol-Tatars, but to the character of their new state system. Military activity and mixed marriages, along with low numbers of Mongol migrants, aided the process of assimilation of the conquerors by the local ethnos. This was noted by an Arab contemporary: "This realm once belonged to the Kipchaks. After the Tatars overran it and subjugated them, over time they mixed and intermarried with [the Kipchaks], whereby the land prevailed over [the conquerors'] nature and essence; they came to be just like the Kipchaks" (al 'Umarī, 1968:235). By the middle of the fourteenth century the Mongol language was no longer the vernacular, but it was retained by the court and in the chancellory records. After 1380 the court was Turkified also: "The Chingisids became Turkic" (Grigor'ev, 1981:82).

The center of the Kipchak state was the Volga basin. There, along its banks, three cities grew, and each in turn became the khan's headquarters: Bolgary (in pre-Mongol times one of the chief cities of Volga Bulgaria), Sarai al-Makhrusa (the Palace Preserved by God), and Sarai al-Dzhedid (the New Palace, also known as Sarai Berke). Altogether in the realm there were at least 110 cities, of which 17 minted their own coins.

Sarai al-Makhrusa was founded by Batu-khan in the early 1250s. Archaeologists have been studying the remains of the city on the left bank of the Akhtuba River near Astrakhan for many years (Fedorov-Davydov, 1984). It was founded as an administrative center, but the first coins were minted there only from 1282. Contemporaries estimated the area of the town as approximately 10 square kilometers. Sarai, noted the Moroccan traveler Ibn Battúta, "is one of the finest of towns, of immense extent and crammed with inhabitants, with fine bazaars and wide streets. One day we walked across the breadth of the town, and the double journey, going and returning, took half a day, this too through a continuous line of houses, with no ruins and no

Manuscript fragment. Birchbark. From a grave near the settlement of Ternovka, middle Volga, early fourteenth century. 13 by 17.5 centimeters. GE 30.402. Hermitage, Leningrad.

A dialog in verse between a son and his mother, who is sending the boy off to serve a feudal lord, is written on birchbark in the Mongol language and Uighur script.

OPPOSITE

Paitza. Silver, gilt. Village of Grushevka. 28 by 9 centimeters. GE 30.295. Hermitage, Leningrad.

The Chinese word "paitza" was used in the Mongol-Tatar states to designate a metal plate issued to officials of various ranks and most often serving as a diplomatic passport. The inscription on the plate indicated the authority of the person who presented it. Highly placed officials had a silver gilt paitza; lower ranks received a bronze paitza. In many cases the paitza simply served as a pass to enter the palace.

This paitza, which was found by chance in 1848 not far from modern Dnepropetrovsk, bears the name of 'Abd Ullah, the ruler of the Golden Horde from 1362 to 1370. The Uighur inscription proclaims: "By the power of eternal heaven [and] by the patronage of great grandeur and magnificence. Who does not submit to the command of 'Abd Ullah, [that] person is guilty [and] will die" (translated by D. Banzarov).

orchards." In the city, which had as many as 75,000 inhabitants, lived Mongols, Alani, Kipchaks, Cherkess, Russians, and Greeks; "each group lives in a separate quarter with its own bazaars" (Ibn Battúta, 1929:165–66). Archaeological excavations have revealed densely packed buildings, the remains of waterpipes and sewers, and palace complexes built out of baked bricks. Sarai al-Makhrusa was a major craft center, where potters, bone-carvers, metal-workers, and jewelers lived and worked. One workshop, which produced glazed pottery and architectural tiles, occupied an area of hundreds of square meters.

Unlike the other cities of the Golden Horde, the God-Preserved Sarai justified its name: although Timur ravaged the state in 1395, the city was still carrying on active trade in the first third of the fifteenth century; in 1433 a Persian merchant sold goods worth 21,000 dinars there at a profit of 50 percent—with the money realized, he bought raw silk, satin, cloth, and Russian linen on the local market (Zakhoder, 1967:166–167). When the city perished is unknown, but its life probably came to a halt with the desolation of the Kipchak state in the second half of the fifteenth century.

The remains of the second capital, Sarai al-Dzhedid or New Sarai, are located not far from modern Volgograd.[2] The city was founded in the early 1330s and continued to grow until 1395 when it was totally destroyed by Timur's armies.

Uzbek-khan, the founder of the city, is buried there. Like the other cities of the Golden Horde, New Sarai at first had no protective walls. The moat and rampart, built only in the years of the stormy feudal internecine strife of the 1360s, at first covered an area of about two square kilometers and included only the central quarters of the capital. As archaeological investigations begun in the last century have shown, New Sarai was an extremely well-built city: it had a complex network of hydrotechnical installations to regulate the level of water in reservoirs. A characteristic feature of its plan was its arrangement by quarters or estates; the nucleus of the city consisted of a few major aristocratic estates. Glassmakers, bronze-founders, copper-workers, bone-carvers, and potters worked in the city, as objects found in the excavations of New Sarai demonstrate. Judging by coin dies, the transfer of the capital from God-Preserved Sarai to New Sarai took place in the reign of khan Dzhani-bek (1341–1357). The rapid growth of the city in its seventy-year existence is evidence of the Golden Horde's great economic potential that was disrupted by Timur's invasion.

The Golden Horde's connection to Khorezm (from 1220 to 1379) and Egypt had a decisive significance in the development of its culture. In 1263 the Sultan of Cairo informed khan Berke (1257–1266) of his "acceptance of nationality

Belt. Gold. Gashun Usta site, north Caucasus, late thirteenth or early fourteenth century. Reconstructed length 110 centimeters. GE Kub 705-721. Hermitage, Leningrad.

The seventeen pieces of this belt include a charm bearing the heraldic crest of the house of Batu, indicating that the first owner of the belt was a member of the family of Batu-khan, Chingis-khan's grandson and founder of the Golden Horde. The images depicted on the individual pieces of the belt show a mix of cultural elements typical of the decorative arts of the period; for example, the plaque with the figure of a deer and flowering trees has a known prototype in east Asian tradition (the Jürchen culture of the late twelfth century), and the Arabian flower reflects the influence of southwest Asian crafts.

BOTTOM

Filigreed ornaments. Gold. North Caucasus, fourteenth century. 2.6 centimeters in diameter. GE Kub 415, 417, 419. Hermitage, Leningrad.

These gold filigreed ornaments were found by chance by peasant treasure-hunters in the Kuban district of northern Caucasus. This type of ornament is typical of those from the Golden Horde that have made their way into museums in Moscow, Leningrad, Baghdad, and Kuwait. The small filigreed stars closely resemble ornaments from Asia Minor, but they are also indisputably linked to the artistic tradition of jewelry from Bukhara and the Crimea.

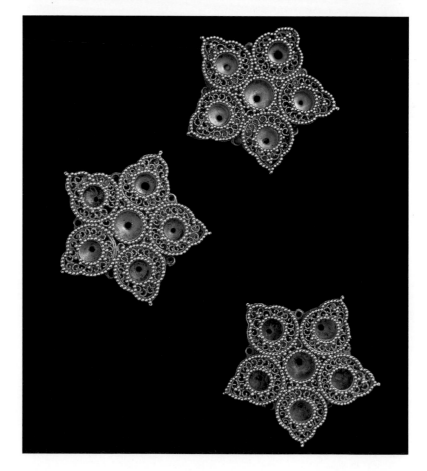

Detail of saber. Steel with gold inlay. Volga region, site of find unknown, 1312 to 1340 A.D. GE 30.56. Hermitage, Leningrad.

The saber bears the gold-incised name Özbeg in Arabic letters, suggesting that the saber may have belonged to Uzbekkhan (1313–1341), the ruler of the Golden Horde who energetically propagated Islam throughout his realm.

and submission"; the connection between the sultanate and the Golden Horde lasted until the total disintegration of the Kipchak state in the first third of the fifteenth century (Polyak, 1964:29). The political connection with Muslim countries permitted the penetration of Islam into the Golden Horde. Already in the reign of Berke, who had been converted to Islam before he took the throne, the conversion of the central regions had begun. "Berke," as the fourteenth-century Arab historian Ibn-Khaldun informs us, "began to build mosques and academies...and brought in scholars and jurists." And although Berke's successors continued to be pagan, the acceptance of Islam had important consequences for both the internal life of the Golden Horde and its international relations at the end of the thirteenth and throughout the fourteenth centuries.

The next step in the spread of Islam through the Kipchak steppes was taken in Uzbek's reign (1312–1342). In 1314 he informed the sultanate about the extension of the dominance of Islam "from China to the farthest outposts of the western states." The introduction of Islam was met with opposition in the nomadic Turkic-Mongol environment, but mosques, *madrasahs* (religious academies), caravanserai, baths, and mausoleums were built in the cities. A few major structures from that time have been preserved to the present day. They give us an idea of the architectural styles and decorative principles developed by the Golden Horde in the last third of the thirteenth and the early fourteenth centuries.

Along with borrowings from the Muslim countries, many traits that originated in the cultures in eastern Asia can be traced in the city plans, architecture, and house construction in the Jochid state. The eastern influence was expressed in the design of certain wooden structures and in the use of a square plan in houses and of heating systems under the floor (a Chinese invention). The nomadic tradition was represented by yurts set up under the palace walls in the capital. But overall, the principles of the decorative systems of Iran, although they were often supplemented by east Asian traditions, dominated. These Near Eastern styles were evident in the exterior appearance of the cities, where the polychrome of mosaics, majolica, and terra-cotta fretwork reigned on the facades, and cobalt dishware was used inside palaces and ordinary dwellings.

The new culture of the Islamic-influenced cities fully corresponded to their new form. The famous doctor from Khorezm, Noman al-Din, who was a scholar of logic and dialectics, lived in Sarai (Uzbek-khan himself often visited him). Judging by the fragments of astrolabes and quadrants found there, the inhabitants of the quarters of the capital knew astronomy and geodesy. The mixture of cultural traditions was evident in language as well. In the fourteenth century a literary language called "Volga Turkic" developed in the cities of the eastern and western parts of the Kipchak state. In 1391 Saifi Sarai translated the *Gulistān* by Sa'dī from Persian into "Turkic." Persian verses made their way out of the narrow circles of intellectuals into the common quarters of the city: lines of verse were inscribed on architectural tiles, vessels, and jewelry. For a while the Mongol language retained its importance also. A unique manuscript on birchbark (early 14th c.) is an interesting relic of the Mongol written language. In Uighur script, it records the verse dialog between a woman and her son, who is leaving for service with a feudal lord. In response to his mother's words of lament, the young man speaks of his attachment to his home, friends, and native steppes (Poppe, 1941).

Vessels and ornaments made of precious metals and meant for a nomadic aristocracy that was ethnically homogeneous had a special place in the culture of the Jochids. Equipment for horses and weapons, ornaments on the warriors' belts, and portable bowls—all the things that served as the "visiting card" of the horseman—took on new meaning in the mid-thirteenth century. The traditional ornaments became stylistic indicators of the degree to which the Turkic majority of common horsemen had assimilated the artistic norms of their Mongol conquerors. Under these conditions toreutics—the art of metal relief—became a leading art form, a heightened representation of the distinctive character of the new style that we now regard as the steppe component of the artistic culture of the Golden Horde. The other Mongol states never developed an art with these distinctive traits because the nomadic Mongols in Iran and China remained a foreign element in the midst of the predominantly urban and agricultural environment.

Ornamental metal work from the 1240s to the 1300s most fully represents the close interaction of several traditions. The era of Chingis-khan with its particular cultural syncretism is evidenced first by the numerous heraldic depictions of dragons on officers' belts and belt buckles. Their imperial symbolism evidently originated as far back as the art of the Ch'i-tan Liao Empire, in which depictions of dragons are found on the ornaments of horses' headgear. This east Asian component entered organically into the artistic symbolism of early Jochid metalwork. Imperial iconography gradually disappeared toward the end of the thirteenth

and first half of the fourteenth century. At that time west Islamic decorative subjects with rudiments of the scenes of animal hunts characteristic of the Near East replaced the east Asian ones. Silver vessels of the Middle Jochid period combined east Asian elements that had crossed the steppes with decorative elements from the urban centers lying between the Muslim East and the Catholic West (Kramarovskii, 1973). From the second half of the fourteenth century, steppe metalwork tended to repeat basic shapes and ornamental motifs of the earlier period.

At this time the art of casting silver objects began to develop in the cities of the Crimean Riviera, where, under the influence of contacts with Italians, craftsmen adapted elements of a Gothic style coming from the island and coastal centers of Latin Romania (Kramarovskii, 1985:152–180).

The cultural life of the Golden Horde took shape in complex and various ways. The rich traditions of the nomadic steppes, quite diverse in their sources, combined with the esthetically expressive craftmanship of the cities to create a distinct and fascinating culture, which, however, has remained unexplicated from the times of Niccolo and Marco Polo, father and son, and still awaits discovery by European civilization. Acquaintance with the culture of the Mongol states could possibly lead to a new understanding of some traits of European culture. As Richard Hennig noted, "the 150-year period during which the danger of a Mongol invasion hung like a storm cloud over Europe also had a most important influence on the Christian world's trade in the thirteenth and fourteenth centuries as well as on the exchange of cultural values" (Hennig, 1953:94).

NOTES

1. The state headed by the inheritors of the house of Jochi was called the Ulus of Jochi in eastern sources; it consisted of two parts—the White Horde and the Blue Horde. The name "Golden Horde," which came from later Russian chronicles, applied to only the western part of the state—the White Horde. However, in scholarly literature Golden Horde is often used to mean the entire state of Jochi, and it is used in that sense here.

2. Sarai al-Dzhedid is sometimes called "Sarai Berke" in archaeological literature and museum documentation. Recent excavations at the Tsarevskoe site, however, have demonstrated that Sarai al-Dzhedid was built after, not during, Berke-khan's reign. The site of Sarai Berke has not been located.

Folk Culture of Eurasian Nomads,
Nineteenth and Twentieth Centuries

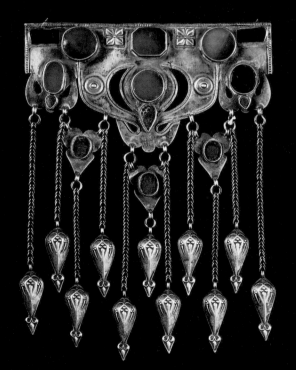

◁ **Buryat woman.** Irkutsk oblast, 1905. Photograph courtesy of Peter the Great's Museum of Anthropology and Ethnography, Leningrad.

Yakut women. Early twentieth century. Photograph courtesy of Peter the Great's Museum of Anthropology and Ethnography, Leningrad.

TOP
Kazakh family. Alma-Ata, 1980s. Photograph courtesy of TASS.

BOTTOM
Kazakh children. Semipalatinsk oblast, Pavlodar region, 1906. Photograph courtesy of State Museum of Ethnography, Leningrad.

OPPOSITE
Turkmen couple. Near Mary, early twentieth century. Photograph courtesy of Peter the Great's Museum of Anthropology and Ethnography, Leningrad.

Eurasian nomads. Nineteenth and early twentieth centuries.

OPPOSITE

Turkmenian elder. 1970s. Photograph by
Yu. A. Argiropulo.

Yurts, Rugs,
and Felts

Vladimir N. Basilov and Ol'ga B. Naumova

Classical authors, writing about the Scythians and Huns, noted that their houses, made "from withes" and covered with felt, were carried on wagons from place to place during their migrations. However, the early nomads, who had retained many traditions of a semisettled life, had other dwellings besides transportable ones. The petroglyphs from Mount Boyary (on the banks of the Enisei in Siberia), which date from the eighth to seventh centuries B.C., depict homes of permanent construction, including some built with logs (Devlet, 1976). That the nomads knew how to erect log structures is attested by archaeological finds in the graves of the Scythian and Sakian aristocracy. It is clear that the early nomads, in addition to their transportable homes, used a variety of dwellings, both permanent and temporary, made from logs, stone, turf, soil, withes, and other local materials.

In the late Middle Ages the yurt, a structure that could be transported even without wagons, became the basic dwelling of the nomads. One distinctive feature of the yurt is its collapsible framework consisting of a standard set of basic components: (1) the trellislike frame (Kazakh: *kerege*) that forms the circular wall; (2) the poles resting on the top of the wall, which formed the main body of the dome (Kazakh: *uïq*); and (3) the cap of the dome (Kazakh: *shangïraq*), which is strengthened by two curving crosspieces. The wooden door, supported in a collapsible wooden frame, is a comparatively recent innovation that replaced a felt flap opening. The most complex element of the yurt is the lattice frame, which is made of separate panels called "wings" (Kazakh: *qanat*). Each panel is composed of overlapping slats that cross at more or less right angles and are joined at points of intersection by leather straps in a way that permits the frame to pivot in correspondence with changes in height. The short slats projecting from the top of the wings are called "heads" (Kazakh: *bas*); there are 15 or more heads in each wing (Mukanov, 1981:26).

The yurt is assembled by first setting up the door in its frame. The wings are then set in place, one at a time, moving clockwise to form a circle. The junctures of the wings are firmly bound with wool tapes, and the first and last wings are attached to the door frame. The dome cap is lifted up on a long stick; the upper ends of three or four dome poles are thrust into the rim of the cap, and their lower ends are attached to the "heads" of the wings. Then the stick is

Scythian petroglyphs. Mount Boyary region, Enisei Basin. These drawings from the eighth or seventh century B.C. testify to the diversity of dwellings known at that time. From Devlet, 1976.

OPPOSITE

Kazakhs. Circa 1937. Photograph courtesy of Peter the Great's Museum of Anthropology and Ethnography, Leningrad.

PAGE 96
Kirghiz. Summer grazing pastures, 1970s. Photograph courtesy of TASS.

removed, and the central roofpiece of the yurt remains supported by the dome poles. Then the remaining dome poles (by Kazakh tradition, there should be slightly fewer of them than of the "heads" of the wings) are connected to the rim of the roof cap. The finished framework is covered with felt rugs. Experience over the centuries proved that a yurt of average size (among the Kazakhs and Karakalpaks, one made of six wings) can be covered by three felt rugs on the walls and two on the dome. A special piece of felt covers the dome cap; it is fastened so that it can be folded open in good weather. The yurt is assembled in a fixed order that makes the work much easier. The work of setting up and dismantling the yurt is done by women. Two women can assemble a yurt in two hours if a man helps to lift the dome cap, and the women can take it apart in even less time. Two or three camels or three or four horses can transport all the pieces of the yurt.

Paucity of sources makes it difficult to establish when the yurt first appeared. It has been suggested that the yurt was invented in the Turkic environment in the middle of the first millennium A.D. (Vainshtein, 1976). Some scholars think that a dwelling similar to the yurt was being used in the Scytho-Sakian era (Kuz'mina and Livshits, 1987). It is probable that different forms of light structures made of wooden frames and felt rugs were widely known in prehistoric

times; the mobile way of life always demanded a dwelling that could be transported to new places and erected in a brief time with little expenditure of effort. A dwelling with the outline of a yurt is depicted in a painting in a Crimean crypt that dates from the third century B.C.

The merits of the yurt are obvious: simplicity of construction, ease of assembly and disassembly, and convenience in transporting. Nevertheless, when we look at the life of the nomads more closely, we see that the yurt coexisted over a long period with earlier forms of dwellings. An Old Russian epic text ("Slovo o polku Igoreve [The Lay of Igor's Campaign]," 12th c.) mentions the "wagons" and *shatry* (evidently, tents) of the Polovtsians. Plano Carpini (13th c.) reported that among the Mongols, "some [dwellings] can be speedily taken down and put up again and are carried on baggage animals; others cannot be taken down but are moved on carts. To carry them on a cart, for the smaller ones, one ox is sufficient, for the larger ones, three, four or even more according to the size" (Plano Carpini, 1955:8). The Kazakhs were still transporting their dwellings by wagon as late as the sixteenth century. Various dwellings with collapsible frames that predated the yurt and were possibly its prototype continued to exist even after use of the yurt became widespread. For instance, some groups of Uzbeks, as well as the Altaians and Jamshids, continued to live in collapsible

dwellings, but their felt walls were held on poles driven into the ground instead of folding wings (Gafferberg, 1948; Karmysheva, 1956).

The nomads were constantly improving the yurt. During the Mongol Empire the yurt had an elongated top—"a neck like a stovepipe" (Rubruck, 1955:91). The Khazars of Afghanistan kept this form of cap (Gafferberg, 1953), while the Turks and Mongols abandoned it. The differences of structure between Turkic and Mongol yurts show that at some point they began to be developed separately. The Mongols preferred the conical dome and used props—one or two poles that supported the cap from inside (evidently, this design is an ancient survival). The Turkic yurt embodied a more elegant solution: the dome was supported without props. The yurt had individual characteristics among different peoples. For instance, the Kazakhs, Kirghiz, and Uzbeks covered the yurt lattice wings with felt rugs over reed matting; the Turkmens put side felts directly over the wings, and the reed mats were fastened on top of the rugs. The Karakalpaks covered the wings only with mats. Among some groups of Uzbeks and Khazars, the wings were horizontally narrow and the yurt walls were made out of two sets of wings, one over the other.

The assembled yurt was solid. The wings were so firmly lashed together that a yurt covered with felt could be moved from place to place without displacing its parts. The yurt's

Kirghiz loading sections of a yurt. 1950s. Photograph courtesy of Institute of Ethnography, Moscow and Leningrad.

inhabitants had no reason to fear strong gusts of wind if the dwelling was held by ropes to stakes driven into the ground. On the banks of the Syrdar'ya and the Amudar'ya, the Kazakhs used the framework of the yurt as a blind for tiger-hunting. The hunters crawled inside the yurt, lifted it up by stakes attached to the inside, and carried it with them as they tracked tigers. When they got within gunshot range of a tiger, they would let the frame down to the ground. When the infuriated beast attacked the yurt, trying to seize the men, it was met with blows of lances and sabers and pointblank gunshots. Even if the tiger leaped onto the dome of the yurt, the dome rods could bear its weight (Zagryazhskii, 1874:*30*).

The organization of the interior space of the yurt was regulated by time-tested steppe customs. An expert on the Kazakh way of life wrote:

> Everything here was calculated and well thought out; everything had its own fixed place. Each guest and family member knows where he is to sit or lie, because it is not rare for as many as fifty guests to gather in this small lodging, and the host lives there....The left side is hung with a bed-curtain that during the day is tucked up...and let down at night to separate the host's sleeping area from that of household members and guests. A wooden, sometimes iron, bedstead or even felt bedding that can be put away during the

daytime is placed in it. The right side is enclosed by a portable partition of reed matting, which is usually decorated with wool or silk. This is the pantry; all food supplies and dishware are stored there; meat, both raw and smoked, is hung on iron rods with hooks or gnarled wooden poles that stand there also. The meat is hung high to keep it out of the reach of dogs.... Between the pantry and a partition of chests and sacks there is always accommodation for the wife of the owner and her daughters and small children. Between the pantry and the doors the dishware and domestic utensils are kept; a *saba* [a large leather sac for *kumys* or fermented mares' milk] stands in the pantry (Zagryazhskii, 1874:29).

An inaccuracy typical of European observers has crept into this description of the interior of the yurt. The yurt actually is divided by an invisible boundary into two sections, right and left, but the nomad tradition counts not from the door, but from the place of honor in the yurt, the "upper" place (*tör*, as it is still called in Turkic languages) situated on the wall opposite the entry. The right (male) side and the left (female) is reckoned from this point (Vasil'eva, 1984:69). The division of the dwelling into men's and women's sections is known to many peoples; it reflects an archaic view of the structure of the world as consisting, like human society, of two halves (Zolotarev, 1964). Some recent writers have suggested that the yurt was seen as a model of the universe. There is no sound basis for this assumption, but the general principles of the world order were naturally taken into account even in the distribution of living space.

The word "yurt" most likely came into Russian from Tatar. In a number of Turkic languages *yurt* means "camp," "place," "country," or "region," but in Tatar the basic meaning of the word is "house" or "estate." Russians used this borrowed word with feminine ending (*yurta*) as the name of the nomads' demountable dwelling. In Turkic languages the ordinary yurt was generally called the "black house" (Kazakh: *qara üy*); this name evidently dates from the Middle Ages, when it became fashionable on the steppes to cover the yurt with white felts and even saturate them with lime or a powder ground from bones (Rubruck, 1955:91). The "black house," therefore, was the ordinary, not the white or ceremonial, yurt.

The yurt was constructed in various sizes. The nomad aristocracy used yurts with walls framed with twelve, eighteen, or even thirty wings (Margulan, 1964:5–9). When housing for a large number of people was needed, the Uzbeks, Turkmens, and Kazakhs joined two yurts with a common doorway.

The bright patterns on the felt rugs covering the yurt and on the wide woolen bands that braced it gave the dwelling a festive air. The world of traditional art surrounded the people inside the yurt as well. Rugs, sacks, curtains, coverlets, utensils, and dishware all gladdened the eye with colorful designs. The dome poles of the yurts of the Kazakh aristocracy were covered with carvings and silver plaques. The yurt presented by the Kazakh sultan Jangir Bukeev to the Russian Emperor Nicholas I on the occasion of his coronation was a masterpiece of traditional folk art—craftsmen worked on it for about two years.

Felting and carpet weaving were widely distributed throughout the nomadic world. Sheep—the basis of the nomad's economy—produced the large quantities of the wool necessary to develop these industries. Among the Mongols, Mongolic Kalmyks, and Buryats, as well as the Turkic peoples of Siberia—Tuvinians, Khakass, and Altaians—only the production of felts developed; they never wove rugs. The preparation of rugs, including pile rugs and patterned felts, took place in Turkestan (Soviet Central Asia), Asia Minor, the Middle East, central Asia, and the Caucasus.

The time that the peoples of Turkestan began to manufacture woven and felt rugs is still unresolved. From the testimony of Classical authors (Herodotus and Pliny the Elder) these industries were known to the Sako-Massagetic tribes who in ancient times inhabited the territory of Turkestan and south Siberia. Their reports have been confirmed by archaeological finds of felts and rugs in the Altai Mountains (Rudenko, 1968) and Khorezm (Tolstov, 1958). The peoples of Turko-Mongol origin who later lived in the same region made patterned felts but did not know how to weave pile rugs. Evidently, the modern peoples of Soviet Central Asia acquired the skill of pile rug-making from their Iranic predecessors (Moshkova, 1970:12)

It is hard to imagine the daily life of the nomadic and seminomadic peoples without carpets and felts. Convenient to handle and transport, they were indispensable to the nomads. Felts covered the yurts, and their floors were spread with rugs and felts as well as pelts. The entry of the yurt was hung with a rug or felt curtain. Sacks made of the same materials served to

Turkmens making felt. 1960s. Photographs by G. Vasiliyeva (page 102) and V. N. Basilov.

store and transport dishware, clothing, and other domestic baggage. Carpets and felts were used for saddlecloths and covers, horse blankets and covers for camels' heads and humps.

Among the nomadic and seminomadic peoples, the women made the rugs and felts, although the men were involved in some steps in the process. Girls were trained to the craft from the age of seven to nine. Everywhere, making large rugs required mutual cooperation; skilled craftswomen were invited to direct the work. The highest quality wool was used to make rugs, the inferior sorts went into felts. From ancient times dyes of plant and mineral origin were used on the wool. In the 1870s aniline dyestuffs appeared in the markets of Turkestan and began to supplant natural dyes; this significantly lowered the quality of the rugs produced in the area.

There were several ways of making patterned felts.

1. The **rolled-pattern technique,** known to the Turkmen, seminomadic Uzbek, Kirghiz, Kazakh, and Karakalpak peoples. The Turkmens, who were famous for their mastery in the preparation of these felts (Vasil'eva, 1985), laid out a pattern of colored wool and added several layers of undyed wool, which served as the background. Kazakh and Kirghiz women used thin or lightly rolled colored felt for the pattern and laid it on a semiprepared base (Masanov, 1959; Makhova and Cherkasova, 1968). In both techniques hot water was poured over the wool mat, and the mat was rolled up into a bolt, which was rolled back and forth on the ground for several hours to compress the wool.

2. The **mosaic technique,** known only to the Kazakhs, Kirghiz, and seminomadic Uzbeks. Patterns were cut from two pieces of felt of different colors, and the pieces were then sewn together: the piece of one color served as the background, and the other, the foreground pattern. Colored cord that emphasized the ornamental outlines was sewn on top of the seam joining the background to the foreground pattern. The patterned felt derived from this process was superimposed on a felt piece of coarser wool, and the two pieces were quilted together along the outlines of the design. The edges of the rug were bordered with wool cord.

3. The **techniques of appliqué, quilting on felt,** and **patterns applied in colored cord.** These methods were used by the Kazakhs and Kirghiz.

The design patterns of Kazakh and Kirghiz felts were very similar. Their basic element was a horn-shaped scroll called the "ram's horn" or "mountain-goat horn." These scroll shapes were combined into various, sometimes very complex, designs. The designs on patterned felts created by Turkmens usually consisted of a few large

Kirghiz women making felt. 1950s. Photograph courtesy of Institute of Ethnography, Moscow and Leningrad.

OPPOSITE
Kirghiz embroidery. Late nineteenth century. 82 by 61 centimeters. MAE 6951-7. Peter the Great's Museum of Anthropology and Ethnography, Leningrad.

All of the peoples of Turkestan and Kazakhstan practiced the ancient art of embroidery. Originally the work depicted animals, people, and gods, but with the propagation of Islam and its prohibition against the depiction of living creatures, patterns of a vegetable and geometric character began to predominate. As late as the last century, the magic significance behind many of the patterns was still known to those who used them.

medallions in the central field framed by a border. Even today almost all the Turkmen ethnic groups retain their original patterns. A wave-shaped border, known in Khorezm in ancient times, can still be seen in Turkmen and Karakalpak felts (*Narody Srednei Azii 1*, 1962:524).

Horizontal looms of primitive construction, both narrow-beamed and broad-beamed, were used to make rugs. The women spun the rug wool themselves, twisting the thread tightly for the warp and spinning a looser strand for the weft and pile.

There were two ways of making the flat-woven rugs (*palas, kilim*) found among the nomads and seminomads of Turkestan. In one, the pattern was created by using colored threads for the warp with undyed weft threads running through it. In the other, rough undyed wool was used for the warp, and the ornamental pattern was woven with colored weft threads (Antipina and Makhova, 1968; Mukanov, 1979; Moshkova, 1970:39–41).

Woven bands were used to reinforce the dome rods and the felt coverings of the yurt; they were sewn together into palas, sacks for utensils, saddlebags, and horsecloths. In some articles, the Kazakhs, Karakalpaks, and Turkmens combined the flat technique with pile weaves. The design of the central Asian flat-woven rugs is geometric;

Kazakh felt making. Semipalatinsk area, 1907. Photograph courtesy of Peter the Great's Museum of Anthropology and Ethnography, Leningrad.

Felt bag. Twentieth century, Kazakhs. 52 by 45 centimeters. MAE 1753-5. Peter the Great's Museum of Anthropology and Ethnography, Leningrad.

elongated rhombi with scrolls and broken lines are often found.

Pile carpets are not manufactured in every region of Soviet Central Asia. This form of rug-weaving was widely distributed among the Turkmen, Karakalpak, and seminomadic Uzbeks. Among the Kirghiz, pile carpets were made only by representatives of the Ichkilik group, and among the Kazakhs, by inhabitants of the Syrdar'ya basin. However, rugs were used even in regions where they were not produced; these were usually bought in the markets.

Clipped ends of knots tied in each pair of threads of the upper and lower row of the warp created the pile of the rugs. In central Asia two types of knot were used, the double (Turkic or German–*ghiordes*) and the one-and-a-half (Persian–*senne*). The latter was the most widely used. After the knot was tied, the weaver clipped its ends with a knife; as each row was finished, the tufts were evened with scissors. Next the weaver made one or two passes with the weft thread (a single weft pass was characteristic of ancient rugs). A comblike wooden instrument with teeth and a handle was used to compress the weft. Then the process was repeated with a new row of knots. The Turkmen rugs were distinguished by their high quality–their density on average was 2,000 to 3,000 knots per square decimeter for bedding rugs (in separate small products it could be as high as 8,000 knots!). The height of the pile never exceeded 7 millimeters. Among other peoples the carpets were not as dense–400 to 800 knots per square decimeter was usual for Uzbeks and Kirghiz rugs, with a pile height up to 9 millimeters.

The design of most central Asian rugs consisted of a repeated basic pattern on the field framed with a border. Among the Turkmens each tribe had its basic rug pattern or *göl*. The highly stylized, geometric pattern of the *göl*, which today we cannot interpret, possibly once represented a bird of prey–the emblem of the Oghuz tribes (Moshkova, 1946). Other elements of the rug designs (plants, animals, cosmological subjects, etc.) were also so highly distorted by geometric outlines that they are hard to recognize,

although in some cases their probable original meaning is known in the area where the rugs are used. This significant stylization distinguishes central Asian rugs from Iranian and Indian ones.

The color range of central Asian carpets is limited; they include four or five, at most eight, different colors. The basic color is different shades of red; the other colors–deep blue, black, white, orange–play a subsidiary role.

As the nomadic peoples of Soviet Central Asia took up a sedentary way of life, the small felt and woven articles, which had been indispensable on migrations, began to disappear from their lives. But the patterned felts used for coverlets, the palas, and the pile carpets were adapted to the settled life and even now decorate the homes of the inhabitants of Kazakhstan, Uzbekistan, and Turkmenia. Many village families still produce them, although some of the traditional ways of making rugs are gradually disappearing. For instance, Uzbeks no longer make mosaic and embroidered felts but restrict themselves to the production of large felt rugs with a rolled pattern; the range of artistic design of the flat-woven carpets is narrowing (Karmysheva, 1985:263). In some northern areas of Kazakhstan where sheep-raising has been curtailed, felts are no longer rolled.

In Turkmenia both rug-weaving and felt-rolling continue to develop intensively. Today these crafts are spreading to regions where they were previously unknown. Most Turkmenian women know how to make a patterned felt, and in almost every Turkmenian family the women weave large and small rugs, women's bags, seat covers for armchairs and cars, saddles for motorcycles and bicycles, and so forth. Every year in Turkmenia there is a public exhibition of the finest examples of the native art of the rug-weaving women (Vasil'eva, 1974).

The ancient domestic crafts today have been put on an industrial basis. Throughout the central Asian republics there are carpet factories. In Ashkhabad one artistic studio works to develop new carpet patterns. Felt-rolling cooperatives in Kazakhstan use the traditional methods of preparing patterned felts.

Lengths of silk fabric. Early twentieth century, Uzbeks. 317–336 by 60 centimeters. MAE 2920-32, 9, 27, 6. Peter the Great's Museum of Anthropology and Ethnography.

Silk was produced by the sedentary population of Turkestan from earliest times and made its way through the bazaars to the nomads of the steppes. The Turkmens, who led a predominantly seminomadic life, also manufactured silk themselves.

Various methods of dyeing the fabric developed in the cities of Turkestan. A popular one was to bind the threads at regular intervals before dipping them into the dye. The bound spots remained undyed, and there was a gradual transition in shade from the colored area to the natural one.

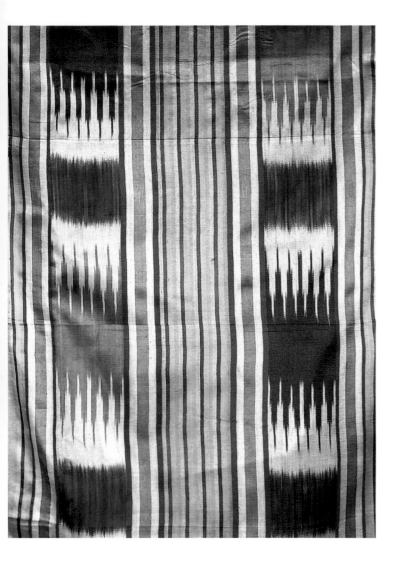

Clothing and
Personal Adornment

Nina P. Lobachëva

In ancient times the nomadic peoples of the Eurasian steppes wore a fixed set of garments in a well-developed style that distinguished them from many sedentary peoples. When Herodotus mentioned that the Sakas had "high caps tapering to a point and stiffly upright…[and] wore trousers" (Herodotus 7.64, 1987:93), he was clearly calling attention to the sort of clothing he found unfamiliar. In his time neither the Greeks nor the Chinese wore trousers. Although we cannot confirm the invention of trousers by the nomads, they certainly played a major role in the widespread dissemination of a garment that was exactly suited to the nomadic life.

The costume of the central Asian Sakas is clearly visible in the famous bas-reliefs of the Achaemenid palace at Persepolis (5th c. B.C.). They wore a sewn garment that extended to the knees and a belt, to which was fastened weapons indicating the wearers' high social position. On their heads they wore *kolpaks*, high pointed hats with flaps over the ears and the nape of the neck; on their feet were high and evidently soft boots (with laces visible on the foot and ankle). On a golden plate from the Amudar'ya trove (4th–3rd cc. B.C.), a Saka is depicted wearing the same costume, with the exception of the headdress, which, judging by its folds, is soft. Evidence from the tomb of the "Golden Man," a Saka aristocrat from Kazakhstan, indicates that he wore a short, close-fitting tunic belted at the waist, narrow trousers, high boots, and a cone-shaped headdress with flaps. A rider depicted on a felt rug

from the Pazyryk graves in the Altai wears a short belted tunic with a lapel on the right side, a standing collar, puffed sleeves tapering to the wrist and bound in narrow cuffs in fabric of a contrasting color; the body of the tunic is embroidered. He has on tight trousers that merge into boots, and a cloak billows at his back. The Scythians living on the south Russian steppes wore a similar costume. We can only marvel that a single costume (with regional variations, of course) was distributed from the shores of the Black Sea to the steppes and mountains of south Siberia.

In the Pazyryk kurgans of the Altai, dating from the middle of the first millennium B.C., and in the Hunnic graves at Kenkol (Kirghizia) and Noin-Ula (Mongolia), from the first years of the Christian era, archaeologists have found the remains of clothing. They give us an idea of the variety of materials the nomads

LEFT

Stone grave marker. Hermitage, twelfth to fourteenth centuries A.D., about 180 centimeters high.

The peaked headdress on the figure, which represents a Kipchak woman, indicates that even in the Middle Ages some Turkic peoples wore headdresses that were very similar to the Kazakh *säukele* of the nineteenth and early twentieth centuries.

RIGHT

Woman's wedding headdress. Fabric, silver. Late nineteenth century, Kazakhs. 191 centimeters long. MAE 523-1. Peter the Great's Museum of Anthropology and Ethnography, Leningrad.

The säukele was a tall conical headdress with pendants at the temples that covered the forehead, ears, and nape of the neck. The base was felt faced with red velvet and decorated with silver plaques and cutout patterns in brocade. Ornaments reminiscent of human figures were fastened to the center and sides of the hat; some scholars see the construction and ornaments of the säukele as symbolic of the "world tree." The forehead piece had otter fur and pendants sewn to it, and the entire headdress was richly jewelled with corals and small pearls. A large triangular veil *(jelek)* made of white Chinese silk was sewn to the back of the headdress.

In the past wealthy Kazakhs decorated the säukele lavishly with silver and precious stones. In the Kazakh folk poem "Kyz-Zhibek" the beautiful heroine elopes with her beloved on the eve of an unwelcome marriage to another; before they leave, she tears the gems off of her säukele and puts them into her pocket.

The säukele was worn for only a short time after its owner married, just until the birth of her first child, and the headdress was then passed down from mother to daughter. In the nineteenth century some of these headdresses were valued at about 1,000 rubles or the price of 100 good horses. By the early twentieth century, the säukele was no longer worn.

OPPOSITE

Kazakh bride with säukele headdress. 1898, southeast Kazakhstan, near Lepsinsk. Courtesy of Peter the Great's Museum of Anthropology and Ethnography, Leningrad.

PAGE 110

Tuvinians. Early twentieth century. Courtesy of Peter the Great's Museum of Anthropology and Ethnography, Leningrad.

General styles of clothing. The clothing of the nomads of the Asiatic steppes in the nineteenth and twentieth centuries can be divided into two general geographical types: Turkestan and Kazakhstan—Kazakhs, Kirghiz, Uzbeks, Karakalpaks, and Turkmens, 1–3 below, and south Siberia—Altaians, Khakass, Tuvinians, Yakuts, and Buryats, 4 and 5. **1–3.** Variants of the "tunic-shaped" garment of Turkestan and Kazakhstan; from Sukhareva, 1979:82. **4.** Variant of a Khakass woman's costume; from *Atlas*, 1961:315, fig. XII 2. **5.** Variant of the cut of a Tuvinian man's costume; from *Atlas*, 1961:318, fig. XV 9.

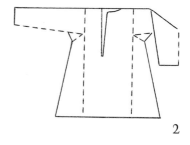

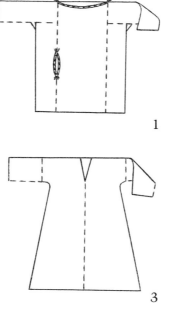

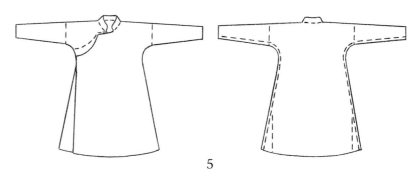

used to make clothing: garments were sewn from plain-weave wool, hempen cloth, silk fabrics, felt, leather, and hides, depending on the purpose of the clothing, the climate, and the social position of the wearer. From the preserved examples of clothing, we can reconstruct its cut and techniques of manufacture, which are very stable elements in a culture. Notwithstanding substantial changes in the look of nomadic costume over the last centuries, many original features of the way various nomadic and seminomadic peoples made their clothing persisted in their traditions until recent times. Archaeological materials from different eras make it possible to follow to some degree the history of the costume of the herding peoples up to the time when ethnographers began studying these nomadic cultures.

The nomadic and seminomadic population of the Asiatic steppes, semideserts, and deserts in the nineteenth and early twentieth centuries can be divided into two large cultural areas with respect to clothing: Turkestan and Kazakhstan, home of the Kazakhs, Kirghiz, Uzbeks, Karakalpaks, and Turkmens, is the first. The other is south Siberia, the land of the Altaians, Khakass, Tuvinians, Yakuts, and Buryats.

The traditional clothing of the peoples of Turkestan and Kazakhstan had a number of traits in common. First, the upper and lower

garments were cut the same way, and the headdresses and footwear were similar. The widely distributed shoulder cut has been called "tunic-shaped" by Soviet ethnographers. The essence of the cut is that the garment was made from a single length of cloth folded in half, so that there were no shoulder seams. The sleeves were sewn to the straight edge of the body piece—that is, the armhole was at a right angle to the shoulder of the garment. Another variant of the tunic cut less frequently seen in that region was one in which the torso and the upper sleeve were cut from a single piece of fabric (this is the cut we find in Hunnic robes from Noin-Ula).

With its roots in deep antiquity, the tunic cut was widely distributed across a broad range of peoples who belonged to different economic and cultural types, spoke different languages, and inhabited the vast territory from the Mediterranean to the Pacific. On the map this area forms a wide band across the middle of the Eurasian continent.

The tunic cut has been described as being of two basic types: (1) a garment worn open in front, the body of which was made from two widths of material, with an obligatory seam down the back, a style characteristic of the peoples of the easternmost areas of the Far East who were primarily agricultural, and (2) a closed garment made from one broad center width with a hole for the head, characteristic of the people of

Woman's dress. Nineteenth century, Turkmens. 138 centimeters long. MAE 6896-1. Peter the Great's Museum of Anthropology and Ethnography, Leningrad.

The Turkmenian women's costume was different from that of the other peoples of Soviet Central Asia and Kazakhstan in cut, color, and ornamental accessories. Turkmenian women wore a long, loose dress with an embroidered placket at the neck that could be dark blue, dark green, or their favorite color, dark red.

OPPOSITE LEFT
Breast ornament. Silver, stamping, relief. Nineteenth century, Kazakhs. 51 centimeters long. MAE 6622-1. Peter the Great's Museum of Anthropology and Ethnography, Leningrad.

RIGHT
Earrings. Silver, coral, stamping, relief, beading. Nineteenth century, Uzbeks. 12.3 centimeters long. MAE 3310-10a, b.

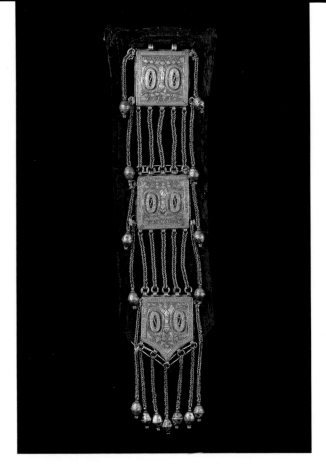

the western periphery of Asia who tended mainly to practice animal husbandry (Sychev, 1977). New data, however, suggest that the earliest tunic-shaped garment was made from two narrow, folded widths of the simplest sorts of plain-woven fabrics. Rudimentary examples of this cut are found in Turkestan, the Volga region, and Southeast Asia.

Evidently the tunic style originated independently at various points on the globe; it might have been connected with the invention of plain-weave cloth, which first made it possible to "tailor" clothing by ripping the fabric along a thread without the use of cutting instruments. Later, the cutting and tapering of cloth led to greater variation and sophistication in the construction of garments. The connection between a well-established complex variant of this cut and the traditional clothing of particular ethnic groups is evidently a later phenomenon. For instance, a tuniclike garment with a wide attached skirt and a curvilinear cut on the breast, wrapped over the right side, became common, as Sychev notes (1977), among the peoples of the *taiga* and forested steppes of south Siberia. The complexity of this style suggests its later origin.

In the nineteenth century a tunic-shaped garment made from one broad central width with supplementary pieces under the sleeves predominated among the peoples of Turkestan and Kazakhstan, in both men's and women's open and closed garments. In this style the sleeves, which narrow to the wrist as the side pieces get broader at the bottom, as well as the extra gores for the body pieces, were cut diagonally with a knife or scissors.

Oblique cuts were also used in the cut of the trousers that men and women alike wore in the nineteenth century. But here, as in the upper garment, there are traces of the style that resulted from ripping the fabric along a thread. In Turkestan we find the type of two-piece leggings (unjoined trousers) that are seen in other regions as well (a Chinese specimen was found at Noin-Ula; it must have been the original style from which this type of clothing developed).

The clothing of the nomadic and semi-nomadic peoples of Turkestan and Kazakhstan was similar in composition as well as cut. The man's costume included a tuniclike open or closed shirt worn next to the body, loose trousers, and a robe with a chemise under it. The camisole appeared in Turkestan only in the nineteenth century. Its distinctive trait was an entirely new cut that followed the lines of the body: the sleeves, sides, and back were all cut out separately, often along curved lines. There was always a seam at the shoulder. The Kazakhs and Kirghiz began using this cut to some extent in the nineteenth century even for their traditional robes: sometimes they made a sleeve with a rounded armhole sewed into the seamed shoul-

LEFT
Coat with false sleeves. Pazyryk kurgans, south Siberia, fifth or fourth century B.C. About 100 centimeters in length. GE 1685/11. Hermitage, Leningrad.

RIGHT
Woman's headcovering. Fabric, embroidery. 1980s, seminomadic Uzbeks. 86 centimeters long. MAE 6952-22. Peter the Great's Museum of Anthropology and Ethnography, Leningrad.

Among the nomads there is a tradition of upper garments with false sleeves, as the coat at left demonstrates. Close examination of the garment at the right reveals that it is embroidered with magic patterns even in the section covered by the joined sleeves, which suggests that in the past the sleeves were not sewn together but hung freely.

In ancient times, the false-sleeved robe was worn over the shoulders; the custom of using this type of garment over the head probably originated in the Middle Ages.

der. The chemise did not catch on among the Turkmens. The costume was finished off with a belt worn over the chemise or robe.

The men wore headdresses of fur or cloth with a fur edging. They also had caps of felt and cloth (for example, the four-gored kolpak with turned-up edges and cloth trim). A skull cap was always worn under the cap. All the peoples of the region used the rainproof robe made from homespun camel's hair and a sheepskin coat.

The women wore a set of garments similar to the man's: a dress next to the skin, trousers, and a robe. The chemise and sleeveless jacket became popular in the nineteenth and twentieth centuries, except among the Turkmens, who rarely wore them. The women's headdresses usually consisted of several components that vividly expressed the ethnic identity as well as the social status and age of the wearer.

An interesting element of the female costume of Turkestan and Kazakhstan is the headcovering that looks like a robe with false sleeves. Turkmens, Karakalpaks, and seminomadic Uzbeks had cloaks like these, and Kazakh and Kirghiz women wore similar garments inside the home. This head-cloak, including the *paranji* of the urban Tadzhik-Uzbek population, is found only in Soviet Central Asia. It is evidently a recent innovation: it does not appear at all in medieval miniatures and is mentioned in written sources only in the eighteenth century.

The coincidence in names and style between the cloaks worn over the head and ordinary shoulder garments indicates that the cloaks developed from older styles. Certain types of robes worn by a number of the peoples of central Asia changed from sleeved garments into cloaks as late as the early twentieth century; modern Turkmens and Uzbeks have cloaks with sleeves that have completely lost their utility and become a decorative detail. It is possible that ancient ceremonial garments worn like cloaks with decorative sleeves served as prototypes. As archaeological evidence shows, already in antiquity some central Asian peoples wore their robes like cloaks tossed over their shoulders. Of course, the abandonment of sleeves might also have been due to a change in the function of the clothing.

In the eighteenth and nineteenth centuries head-cloaks became an obligatory element of everyday streetwear. What led to the appearance of such an original garment? Ancient beliefs in the necessity of hiding women from the effect of harmful forces at important moments in life (for instance, at a wedding when the bride was brought to her new husband's house) may have been reinforced by the Muslim tradition of concealing women from the gaze of strangers. The most extreme embodiment of this concept was the Tadzhik-Uzbek paranji that had an additional net made of black hair (chachvan) to cover the face. It was evidently the example of the paranji that led to the custom among some other peoples of Turkestan and Kazakhstan of requiring women to wear a head-covering cloak outside the home.

A devotion to robes made of striped fabrics with little metal ornaments, usually from silver, sewn onto them was a general trait among the peoples of Turkestan and Kazakhstan. Richness of fabric and ornament in clothing and the number of garments worn marked social rank. A rich belt with accessories was a sign of high social status for men. Dress for ceremonial occasions was not marked by variation in style; instead, color and a fixed combination of garments marked the costume's function. The age of the wearer often dictated the color of the fabric from which the costume was sewn.

These common traits in the appearance of clothing developed as a result of the constant links among the peoples of Turkestan and Kazakhstan over the millennia. In turn, there were two distinct variants of costume among these same peoples: The costume of the Kazakhs, Kirghiz, Karakalpaks, and seminomad Uzbeks of the Kipchak steppe was distinct in a number of elements from that of the Turkmens. The character of these differences was connected with the peoples' historical fates and their degree of kinship and common cultural community. Some of the differences corresponded to differences in language: the Kazakhs, Kirghiz, and Karakalpaks spoke languages from the Kipchak group of Turkic languages, while the Turkmens' language belonged to the Oghuz group.

A number of distinctive elements were characteristic of the female costume of the first type. For instance, the headdress called in Kazakh the säukele–a tall conical hat (the shape varies with different peoples) richly ornamented with silver and coral beads–was worn by the Kazakh, Kirghiz, and Karakalpak marriageable girls and young married women on ceremonial occasions. (Stone grave monuments left by the Polovtsians in the south Russian steppes in the twelfth to fourteenth centuries are evidence that Kipchak women wore a high headdress like a säukele or kolpak even in the Middle Ages.) Typical of the Kazakhs and Kirghiz is an obligatory element of the women's headdress called the kimeshek–a distinctive cowl with an aperture for the face, which a woman wore on her wedding day. The traditional Kirghiz women's costume featured a richly embroidered wrapped skirt on a broad belt, the bel'demchi; Kazakh women also wore this garment.

Distinctive traits of the male costume included suede trousers with chain-stitch embroidery for the warriors and young men and a belt, the kemer, with metal plaques sewn on leather or thick cloth. The felt kebenek (cloak) was very typical of shepherd's clothing, as was a felt or cloth kolpak with four gores and colorful flaps (the Kazakhs wore white kolpaks decorated with embroidery).

A woman's headdress with a rigid frame and often with a flat top, which in the old days was high and heavy with massive silver ornaments, is characteristic of the second variant– the Turkmen costume. Turkmen women liked roomy dark-red dresses with rich embroidery on the collar; their trousers were decorated with broad embroidered cuffs. There was a striking abundance of silver jewelry. Outer garments varied in shape. There was a noticeable partiality to clothing in lush colors of the same tonality combined in attractive ways. A red veil was thrown over the headdress, and when men were present the Turkmen women covered the lower half of their faces with the edge of their shawl. Girls wore a unique headdress, a skull cap with a silver centerpiece that made it look like a helmet.

The typical Turkmen male costume included a large deep-piled sheepskin cap, a white closed shirt with a shoulder opening, trousers that were loose in the seat and comparatively tight across the legs, and a robe made out of red-and-blue striped cloth.

Despite the similarities, the costume of each people was distinctive. A Kazakh girl could be recognized instantly from her light-colored flounced dress, dark velvet camisole or sleeveless jacket, and her cap with its fur trim and plume of eagle-owl feathers. The headdress of the married Kazakh woman consisted of a white kimeshek edged with embroidery and topped by a light-colored turban whose shape varied with different Kazakh groups. The Kirghiz women's headdress, the *elechek*, was easily distinguished from that of the Kazakhs. It was always white and folded in numerous neat rows around the head. The Karakalpak kimeshek was made out of cloth of a color determined by the age of the wearer, white for an elderly woman, red for a young one. The part of the kimeshek that covered the breast was in red fabric with a black stripe in the middle; it was almost all covered with embroidery in a geometric design. Each ethnic group had its own type of men's headdress.

The costumes of the peoples of south Siberia are significantly different from those of Turkestan and Kazakhstan and show less uniformity. Several cultural traditions can be traced, most clearly in outer garments and headdresses. One of these traditions is adaptation of the tunic style; the clothing of the northern Altaians, for instance, was based wholly on the tunic-shaped cut. Another tradition was retention of the type of tunic style in which the upper sleeves and torso were cut from one broad single or seamed width, and the left side of the front was further broadened by an extra length of fabric sewn to its vertical selvage. The left side had a curved neckline, folded over the right to cover the front of the body, and fastened under the sleeve and at the shoulder. The Tuvinians, Buryats, and Mongols wore outer garments of this type, which was known to the Huns, as finds at Noin-Ula show.

A third traditional style not found in Kazakhstan and Turkestan was a garment with seams at the shoulders and an armhole cut generously in back (the sleeve seams followed two symmetric curved lines along the back of the

Woman's robe and sleeveless jacket. Fabric, mother-of-pearl ornaments. Early twentieth century, Khakass. 149 centimeters long. MAE 5060-19, 335-1. Peter the Great's Museum of Anthropology and Ethnography, Leningrad.

The Khakass women's summer robe *(sikpen)* was usually lined with lightweight black cloth. The collar, of brightly colored brocade or blue or red velvet, was decorated with mother-of-pearl disks and metal plaques. The sikpen was always worn on holidays and ceremonial occasions. By the late nineteenth century, its use as a rule was confined to well-to-do herders in the steppe zone of Khakassia.

The sleeveless jacket, or *sigedek,* was always worn by married Khakass women. Girls prepared their wedding clothing—fur coat, sleeveless jacket, headdress, and a set of accompanying jewelry—well in advance and with great skill. Women made one jacket to last a lifetime. The armholes and collar bore embroidered figures, and the body had silk tassles, mother-of-pearl buttons, and braid. In cold weather the jacket was worn over a fur coat. Young women wore it whenever they took part in ceremonies and at weddings in particular. A local variant of the sigedek was part of the women's costume of the Altaians, Yakuts, Buryats, and Mongols also.

OPPOSITE TOP
Turkmen girl. Tashauz oblast, 1969. Photograph by V. N. Basilov.

OPPOSITE BOTTOM
Girl's headdress. Fabric, silver. Early twentieth century, Turkmens. 21 centimeters in diameter. MAE 5309-17. Peter the Great's Museum of Anthropology and Ethnography, Leningrad.

Girls' headdresses like this one are traditional only in Turkmenia and can still be seen there today. The basic ornament of the cap was the metal dome-shaped top piece *(kupba)* with a little tube projecting from it. In earlier days feathers from an owl, eagle, or falcon, which were considered talismans, were worn in the kupba. The lower part of the cap was covered with silver coins, and pendants hung from the temples. That the outline of the cap resembles a helmet may not be entirely coincidental: it is possible that centuries ago, when martial raids were considered feats of valor, the girls' caps were deliberately made in the shape of helmets.

When a Turkmenian girl married, this headdress was replaced by that of a wife. Wearing a cap with no feathers in it was a sign of betrothal.

Yakut women serving kumys. Early twentieth century. Photograph courtesy of Peter the Great's Museum of Anthropology and Ethnography.

OPPOSITE RIGHT
Woman's bracelets. Metal. Nineteenth century, Yakuts. 12.5 centimeter high. MAE 4282-109/2. Peter the Great's Museum of Anthropology and Ethnography, Leningrad.

Yakut girls and women usually wore bracelets whose surface was covered with engraved geometric and vegetable patterns. The copper and silver of such ornaments was thought to protect the wearer from the evil eye and other troubles.

garment). This cut created broad, sometimes puffed, sleeves and sometimes allowed for a gathered "flounce" of skirt to be added at the back, seamed at the waist. The outer garments of the Khakass and Yakuts were most representative of this style.

The peoples of south Siberia who retained nomadic traditions in their culture into the twentieth century combined these styles in different ways to create a variety of garments (Atlas, 1961). There were two basic types of collar: stand-up (Altaians, Tuvinians and Buryats) and turned-down (Khakass and Yakuts; occasionally Altaians). Costume specialists see the Altai as the boundary between the two regions. Different cultures met and mixed in the Altai from ancient times; the clothing found in the Pazyryk kurgans is distinguished by a wide variety of styles.

The way in which garments were combined in costumes is also noteworthy. The summer costume for men and women of the southern Altai included shirt, roomy trousers, and broad tuniclike outer robe. The cut of the women's robes was more complex than those of the men and girls; armholes and sleeves were shaped differently. When married women left their homes, they usually wore a sleeveless garment called a *cheqedek* over the outer robe; it was cut straight in front and consisted of a bodice with wide armholes, which attached to a gathered

skirt slit from the hem to the waist. This garment was not buttoned, but two large buttons were always sewn to the left side. It was even worn over the sheepskin coat that protected the Altaians from the cold and was often worn all summer in the harsh mountain climate. The left side of the sheepskin coat, like that of the robe, was wrapped over the right. Its turned-down collar was usually made of fox fur, and the left side and the hem were trimmed with colt hide. The woman's coat, unlike the man's, was shaped and gathered at the waist. The semicircular cuff of the sleeve, long enough to cover the hand, was trimmed with fur or red cloth. Otter collars were popular.

The caps of both men and women usually featured a cloth crown and a high fur band in front that narrowed in back, where two ribbons were fastened.

A garment like the cheqedek was characteristic of the Khakass culture. They used the cut for all sorts of clothing, and it is quite possible that neighboring peoples borrowed the cheqedek from the Khakass.

The clothing of the Tuvinians was similar to that of the Buryat Mongols. Their summer costume consisted of a shirt, trousers, and a long robe in the tunic style with the left side folded over the right. The women's robes featured a wide flounce at knee level. The Tuvinians also had a sleeveless garment like the cheqedek.

Like the Altaians, the Tuvinians often wore their sheepskin, deerskin, or roe-deerskin coats even in summer. The men's and women's coats were identical: long and somewhat flared at the hem, with straight sleeves. The men tucked the tail of their coats into their belts when they walked. The women's coats, like their caftans, were decorated with a narrow strip of precious fur or varicolored pieces of fabric around the skirt and jutting out at the breast. The conical headdresses with fur trim retained a traditional form.

The traditional Buryat and Mongol costumes were much alike. In the summer they wore a shirt, trousers, and robe made of wool and silk fabrics bought from the Russians and Chinese. The belt was an integral part of the male costume. The eastern Buryats, like the Mongols, used pieces of silk cloth as belts; the western Buryats wore leather belts decorated with ornamental metal plates in the Turkic tradition.

The women's robe required a broad gathered skirt sewn onto the waistline. The armhole was spaciously cut, and the sleeves were also gathered at the shoulder. The collar, the edge of the sleeves, and sometimes the hem were edged with fur or a contrasting color of silk. Over their robes the women wore sleeveless jackets, either waistlength or long, like those of the Tuvinians.

Like the Mongols, the Buryats made their winter coats from sheepskin covered with fabric (for the wealthy, brocade or silk). The coat had a slight flare, and the sleeves' semicircular cuffs covered the hand. The most common headdress for men was a bonnetlike cap of coarse cloth covered with colored silk. They also wore a cap with a conical crown and a broad brim that was slit and turned up in the back. The band was trimmed with fur or black velvet.

The Yakuts were unique among the peoples of south Siberia in that both men and women wore, next to the skin, leather trousers, a fur band covering the stomach, and high leather leggings (like single trouser legs). The cloth shirt appeared later (perhaps under Russian influence, as their word for it—ïrbakhï (from Russian *rubakha*)—suggests).

The outer garments of both sexes were also identical. Unlike their steppe-dwelling neighbors, the Yakuts sewed their clothing with a straight opening down the front (the left side did not fold over the right). The caftan was the most typical outer garment of the Yakuts (cloth for summer and fur in winter). It was made of four wedge-shaped strips sewn together with additional gores in the skirt. The sleeve of the garment had a capacious armhole and was gathered in deep folds narrowing to the cuff. The women's winter caftan featured a squirrel-tail collar. Their holiday dress was ornamented with

Man's robe. Chinese silk. Early nineteenth century, Buryats. 134 centimeters long. MAE 702-7. Peter the Great's Museum of Anthropology and Ethnography, Leningrad.

This robe belonged to a wealthy and influential Buryat prince, or *taisha*, who was the head of several major family groups. A soaring dragon, the symbol of the universe and of limitless imperial power, is depicted on the center of the breast. In China robes like this were worn only by the emperor and members of his family, although representatives of other aristocratic families would array themselves in dragon robes during periods when the imperial power was at its weakest. The Mongols took up the tradition after their conquest of China (thirteenth century), and members of the ruling family of Chingis-khan began to wear robes bearing the imperial dragon. Among the eastern Buryats, who were under strong Mongol influence, members of the aristocracy who laid claim to descent from Chingis-khan also wore Chinese silk robes with dragons on them. Later, when the Buryats joined the Russian empire in the seventeenth and eighteenth centuries, every aristocrat felt free to wear these robes.

strips of precious fur edging the hem and sleeves. Over their outer garments, men wore leather belts decorated with metal plaques.

The Yakuts had a great variety of headdress. The most traditional was evidently a bonnet with a tall conical crown made of fur, suede, or cloth, which was worn by both sexes.

As we see, the nomadic or seminomadic way of life did not require uniformity in dress; on the contrary, there was a rich variety. From ancient times to the Middle Ages there were many changes in the costumes of the steppe animal herders. Some types of garment disappeared and others arose. Diversity in dress arises from difference in historical circumstance. Each people reproduced the established clothing styles and then modified them. Similarity in elements of modified clothing among different peoples indicates that in the recent past they had close ties and a consequent identity in cultural traditions. From the fourteenth to the early twentieth centuries, there was a marked resemblance in the costumes of the peoples of Turkestan and Kazakhstan, and to a lesser degree in those of the peoples of south Siberia.

Man's cap. Fabric. Nineteenth century, Buryats. 31 centimeters high. MAE 6832-7. Peter the Great's Museum of Anthropology and Ethnography, Leningrad.

The Buryat man's headdress always reflected his ethnic (and often family) identity and his social position. In the mid nineteenth century the tsarist administration issued a special decree on Buryat life and customs that reinforced and legislated the differences in dress prescribed for all social levels. Only the eastern Buryats wore headdresses like this one: the dark blue ("sky") color of the silk and the silver gilt tip indicate that the headdress belonged to a commander of high rank or the head of a large Buryat family group *(taisha)*.

BOTTOM LEFT

Shoulder ornaments. Silver, coral, silk. Nineteenth century, Buryats. 12 centimeters long. MAE 1920-9a, b. Peter the Great's Museum of Anthropology and Ethnography, Leningrad.

RIGHT

"Steel" (for fire lighting). Silver. Nineteenth century, Buryats. 44 centimeters long. MAE 313-94. Peter the Great's Museum of Anthropology and Ethnography, Leningrad.

Steels of this type were widely used by both men and women among the Buryats, Mongols, Tuvinians, and Yakuts in the eighteenth and nineteenth centuries. There is a Buryat tradition that in the old days the steels (which probably came into use no earlier than the sixth to eighth centuries A.D.) were used instead of money as a medium of exchange.

Household Furnishings
and Utensils

Vladimir N. Basilov, Vera P. D'yakonova,

Vladimir I. D'yachenko, and Vadim P. Kurylëv

Over the centuries the nomadic herders of the Eurasian steppes developed types of domestic utensils well adapted to their way of life—light, unbreakable objects that could be constantly transported from place to place. The need for such utensils was evidently felt even from ancient times when large wagons were available to carry cumbersome, heavy baggage. In the Middle Ages, when wagons became obsolete, the need for durable and lightweight utensils manufactured from materials at hand undoubtedly increased. During that period, as archaeological materials demonstrate, the nomads stopped making ceramic pots, and the use of metal vessels evidently decreased.

Of course it was impossible to eliminate metal from life altogether; local smiths used it to make weapons, tools, and everyday objects of various sorts—for example, special hooks to lift meat from kettles and perforated ladles. Metal ewers spread along with Islam. Metal kettles for cooking food took on a more convenient shape in the Middle Ages, becoming flatter in shape and losing the cone-shaped support or "feet" permanently soldered to the bottom. At the same time, a new object appeared—a hoop on feet (a trivet) on which the kettle could be set. (Earlier nomads probably used kettles without trivets that were hung over the hearth. In a number of Turkic languages the phrase "to put a kettle on the fire," *kazan asmak*, means literally "to hang a kettle.") The nomads had a few fragile belongings, which they took special measures to preserve. When, because of the interest in rare imported items common to all peoples, the porcelain cup (*piala*) for tea-drinking appeared in the steppes (probably no earlier than the 18th c.), the nomads adapted this foreign fashion to their way of life by making cases out of leather, felt, or wood to carry these precious objects during migrations.

Wood was in general use among the early nomads. A variety of wooden objects—small tables, trays, dishes, and bowls—were found during excavation of *kurgans* (burial mounds) from the Scytho-Sakian era in Kazakhstan and the Altai. Some forms of wooden utensils typical of the early nomads survived into the twentieth century. For example, the Tuvinians still kept liquid-storing kegs shaped almost identically to those of Hunnic times. Little wooden tables and bowls with handles like those that were widely distributed among the Scythians and Sakians were still used by the Ossetians, descendants of the Alani, on the boundaries of the nomadic world, in the northern Caucasus. Nomads and

PAGE 126
Yakut girl. The young woman wears her ceremonial dress and is surrounded by the utensils and dishes used for serving kumys at festivals, 1910. Photograph courtesy of State Museum of Ethnography, Leningrad.

OPPOSITE
Samovar. Metal. Late nineteenth century, Uzbeks. 51.5 centimeters high. MAE 3780-57a, b. Peter the Great's Museum of Anthropology and Ethnography, Leningrad.

In the nineteenth century the Russian samovar became fashionable among the peoples of Turkestan and Kazakhstan; by the end of the century, the samovar was a fixture in the Kazakh yurt. Uzbek craftsmen became proficient at manufacturing them, using traditionally shaped vessels for the body.

LEFT
Tetrahedral bottle. Ornamented leather, wooden stopper. Late nineteenth century, Turkmens. 38 centimeters high. MAE 3325-1a, b. Peter the Great's Museum of Anthropology and Ethnography, Leningrad.

The shape of this vessel is modeled after that of European glass bottles. The techniques of manufacture, however, are the traditional ones used by the nomads through the centuries.

BOTTOM
Bag for transporting kumys. Leather. Late nineteenth century, Kazakhs. 27 centimeters high. MAE 5235-5. Peter the Great's Museum of Anthropology and Ethnography, Leningrad.

Case for cup. Leather. Early twentieth century, Turkmens. 44 centimeters long. MAE 3175-2. Peter the Great's Museum of Anthropology and Ethnography, Leningrad.

Cases like this were used to carry fragile porcelain cups *(piala)* on campaigns and during migrations. To keep the piala safe from jolts, the case was lined with fine felt. The rider usually slung the piala case from his saddle.

OPPOSITE
Kazakh blacksmith. Akmolinsk oblast, 1908. Photograph courtesy of State Museum of Ethnography, Leningrad.

seminomadic peoples everywhere liked to eat from wooden dishes; in central Asia in the nineteenth century these were produced on a simple lathe. Wooden chests used to store clothing and valuable belongings were characteristic of the nomads' way of life. In the thirteenth century such chests, covered with felt "soaked in tallow or ewe's milk so that [they are] rainproof," were essential equipment for the Mongols, who transported them on carts (Rubruck, 1955:94). Even the early nomads probably used boxes of various sizes. Wooden beds, often decorated with carvings and, among the Kazakhs, with bone inlay, were known to some nomadic peoples (Kazakhs and inhabitants of the southern Altai) in the nineteenth and twentieth centuries. Bedsteads are by no means a recent innovation; they were in use by the Middle Ages. Among the Mongols, both the head of the family and his wife had beds on legs (Rubruck, 1955:96).

An important class of objects used by the nomads was sacks and saddlebags designed to preserve and transport belongings and provisions. They were sewn from leather, felt, and durable fabric; in Turkestan sacks made from rugs were also widely used. On a visit to the Altai in the second half of the nineteenth century, W. Radloff wrote: "In some yurts I saw forty or more such sacks. Their contents included clothing, lengths of fabric, rugs, coverlets, pieces of felt, various ornaments, pelts, fur articles, brick tea, bridles for horses, straps and ropes" (Radloff, 1884:1.272).

One of the most remarkable features of the nomads' culture was the abundance of articles made from leather. This is a tradition dating from the most ancient times. In the Scythian kurgans of Tuva and the Altai (7th to 3rd cc. B.C.) leather items have been discovered that are similar in processing techniques and function to those still common in the early twentieth century among the herders of south Siberia, Turkestan, and Kazakhstan. Leather was a versatile material that had practical uses in every aspect of the lives of nomadic and seminomadic peoples.

Leatherware, which was lightweight and durable, was used extensively by the nomads. The peoples of south Siberia customarily presented a bride's parents with flasklike leather vessels at one stage of the matchmaking; as the wedding approached, the bride herself received leatherware from her parents and relatives. Inside the yurt utensils and leather vessels were relegated to the women's section. They were hung from the lattice frame of the yurt by hair-cord loops and brackets.

The herders' processing of leather reached a high level of sophistication by employing only simple specialized tools (mallets, scrapers, knives, etc.). The dressing of the hides, depending on type, was carried out in the family by women as well as men, and children were introduced to the work at an early age. Before a leather vessel or dish was made, the hide was cleaned and kneaded after a preliminary softening in sour milk (a method known at least by the Middle Ages (Rubruck, 1955:103) and evidently much earlier). Then it was smoked for several days to make it long-lasting and water-resistant. The vessel was sewn together from pieces of leather of the proper shape with cords made of sinews of both wild and domestic animals. These cords were durable and were used even by the early nomads of the Eurasian steppes. A vessel

was properly shaped by being filled with damp ash or soil; after it dried, the soil or ash was removed, and the vessel was painstakingly washed with tea with an admixture of salt and grease.

Leather dishes were closely related to the traditional diet of the nomads, in which varied kinds of milk foods—fermented and boiled milk, butter, and cheese—played a major role. During the summer, the months when domestic animals lactated actively, milk was used directly for food and also converted for later use. The milk or liquid milk products were stored mainly in leather vessels.

The nomads well understood the properties of the hides of different animals. The biggest leather vessel, called a *saba* by the Kazakhs and Altai people (and also *arkït* by the Altaians), held up to 185 liters. It was sewn from smoked cow- or horsehide and was used not only for storage but also in the preparation of milk products.

Sour milk ready for use was usually kept in vessels of small capacity (about 18.5 liters). In south Siberia these were made from two pieces of hide from a horse's hindshank. The mouth of the vessel was reinforced with a wooden rim that had a loop for hanging the vessel attached to it. An archaic form of the utensil used this way was a sack *(kalama)* made from a single piece of skin from a horse's head; the holes left by the eyes, ears, and mouth were sewn shut. The kalama is apparently one of the oldest forms of leather vessel.

The Altai and Kirghiz peoples made distinctive small pails out of the udders of cows and Siberian deer, which were used to ladle sour milk from larger vessels and also to store dry provisions. From the scrota of rams and bulls the Altai made vessels to hold tea and salt or women's sewing equipment. Frequently the capacity of these vessels was increased by sewing a piece of fabric or hide from some other organ of the animal (for instance, the udder) to the scrotum. The vessels the nomads made from the internal organs, stomach, and intestines of wild and domestic animals were both distinctive and practical. They were used from earliest times to store provisions for winter, in particular butter and fat.

Flasklike vessels were widely distributed among the Altaians, Tuvinians, Khakass, Kazakhs, and Kirghiz and were used to transport milk drinks. The flasks, which were a necessary attribute of various ceremonial events, were fastened to the horse saddle for holiday visits. Among the Altaians the flasks were used in one of the rites of childhood: a small vessel was made for a little boy and when he turned three he brought it as a sign of respect to his maternal uncle. The flasks were richly ornamented, the work usually carried out by women. A small wooden plaque bearing a carved design was

LEFT

Scoops for pouring kumys. Wood. Late nineteenth century, Kazakhs. 43 by 7 and 37 by 15 centimeters. MAE 3460-1, 1201-1. Peter the Great's Museum of Anthropology and Ethnography, Leningrad.

Wooden scoops for pouring kumys were often in the form of two joined scoops. The origin of this tradition has been forgotten, but one explanation is that the ancients used one half of the scoop to pour kumys dedicated to the sky spirits and the other for those of the underworld.

RIGHT

Cup. Wood with metal incrustation. Early twentieth century, Kirghiz. 13 centimeters high. MAE 6182-1. Peter the Great's Museum of Anthropology and Ethnography, Leningrad.

OPPOSITE

Ceremonial vessel for kumys. Wood. Nineteenth century, Yakuts. 35 centimeters high. MAE 2666-76. Peter the Great's Museum of Anthropology and Ethnography, Leningrad.

Wooden vessels called *choron* were used by the Yakuts to drink kumys during festivals. The choron was always carved from a single piece of wood and came in a range of sizes. The lower part was a conical base or a stand on three or four feet shaped like horses' hooves. During the Yakuts' main festival celebrating animal husbandry *(isïakh)* in spring or early summer, shamans poured libations from the choron in honor of fertility deities and spirits; other festival participants raised the choron on high before drinking and chanted propitiatory prayers to the sky spirits.

The vessel's ritual importance was emphasized by its ornamentation—carving, copper hoops, and noise-making pendants. The designs carved on it are ancient and resemble patterns on ceramic dishes dating from the fifth to second century B.C. found in south Siberia.

placed under the damp leather, and the design was impressed into the hide with a sharpened wooden or bone stick.

The utensils connected with the milk beverage *kumys* that is so typical of the nomadic cultures of the Eurasian steppes deserve an extended description. Kumys is a nourishing and slightly intoxicating beverage of mares' milk. It was known from earliest times; the pastoral peoples may have enjoyed it long before nomadism arose. Herodotus tells us that the Scythians drank mares' milk. "When they have drawn the milk, they pour it into hollow containers of wood. They range their blind slaves about the buckets and get them to shake the milk" (Herodotus 4.2, 1987:279). (This shaking process may be depicted in Scythian petroglyphs from the Boyary Mountains in the Enisei basin.) Rubruck in his account of a visit to the Mongols in 1253–1255 dedicated an entire chapter to the beverage. His information is much more detailed than Herodotus's account:

> The Mongols pour mares' milk into a large skin or bag and they begin churning it with a specially made stick which is as big as a man's head at its lower end, and hollowed out; and when they beat it quickly it begins to bubble like new wine and to turn sour and ferment, and they churn it until they can extract the butter. Then they taste it and when it is fairly pungent they drink it.

Kirghiz making wooden dishware. 1950s. Photograph courtesy of Institute of Ethnography, Moscow and Leningrad.

This is indeed kumys. It "greatly delights the inner man; it even intoxicates those who have not a very good head. It also greatly provokes urine" (Rubruck, 1955:98–99).

Kumys was prepared in the same way that it had been for millennia. Mares were kept specifically for their milk and milked four or five times a day (or even every two or three hours; there were insignificant local variations in the process). Usually the milker stood to the right side of the animal, and the colt was allowed to approach the mare to encourage her to let down her milk. The herders preferred using vessels made of leather or wood, because they thought that the sharp sound of the jet of milk striking the bottom of a metal pail might frighten the animal.

The mares' milk was then poured into a saba or large leather sack. The Kazakh saba was conical in shape and had a broad square bottom; toward the top it tapered to a narrow neck. The saba of wealthy Kazakhs was huge, with a capacity of nearly 500 liters. It took up to ten horsehides to produce. A cord attached to the neck of the saba was used to fasten it to the lattice framework of the yurt—as a rule, to the right of the entrance. The saba sat on a special wooden stand, which, by ancient tradition, was sometimes ornamented with woodcarving, painting, or bone or silver inlay. Rubruck described a Mongol dwelling of the thirteenth century: "Standing in the entrance is a bench with a skin of milk or some other drink and some cups." About another home, he said, "Then we went in. Near the entrance was a bench with some [kumys] on it" (Rubruck, 1955:96, 153).

In a Kazakh or Kirghiz yurt where kumys was being prepared, there was the constant rhythmic sound of the milk being whipped with a special wooden whisk having a flat working part at the lower end. The upper section of the beater was often decorated with an ornament made of antler, bone, or metal. The nomads lived on kumys during the summer months and were accustomed to offer it to everyone who visited the yurt.

The leather vessels in which the Kazakhs, Kirghiz, and Tuvinians stored and transported the drink were distinguished by beauty and elegance of workmanship. They were usually decorated with stamped patterns. The wooden ladles used to pour kumys and the bowls from which kumys was drunk were also made with loving care and usually decorated with carvings and bone and silver inlays. The Kazakhs had a tradition of carving kumys ladles in the shape of two hemispheres with a curved handle.

In ancient times the nomadic peoples considered kumys a sacred drink (for example, it could not be poured on the ground). The festival of new kumys, in which, according to Rubruck, the Mongols consecrated white mares, was celebrated in the spring (Rubruck, 1955:198). This festival is described in more detail in comparatively recent accounts. In the 1770s the German naturalist Peter Simon Pallas wrote about the ceremonial consecration of a horse by the Khakass:

> The chief festival that the Kashintsy, like the other pagan Tatars, celebrate is the spring festival *(tun)* when they begin to milk the mares.... Neighbors gather from various *ulus* in one place and bring out into the open fields, most often to a hill, the ceremonial sacrifice... with festival prayers to the east.... And then they consecrate a horse.... The [horse] so consecrated is resanctified every spring at the time of *tun:* they wash him in milk boiled with wormwood, and they scent him with the same herb, adorn his tail and mane with red and white scraps, and release him to run free (Pallas, 1776:401–402).

Survivals of this spring festival could still be found among the Kazakhs as late as the mid-nineteenth century; Islam had succeeded, however, in eliminating its former religious significance. On the other hand, the holiday retained its original symbolism in Yakut customs even into this century. Among the Yakuts this *isïakh* festival was celebrated with the appearance of the first green shoots and was largely connected with the cult of the horse. It was accompanied by ceremonial poetry, ritual dances, and the shared drinking of consecrated kumys. The festival began with a eulogy of the divinities on whom the parturition of horses and cattle, the harvest, and the health and wealth of the Yakuts depended. At sunrise inside their birchbark yurts the herders held up bowls filled with kumys. The next part of the festival

occurred outside, usually in a large clearing, with a gathering of hundreds or even thousands of people who took seats in a circle. Between two carved posts with finials shaped like a horse head or a kumys goblet was set a huge (up to 550 liters) leather vessel containing kumys. The drink was poured with a carved scoop into large carved wooden bowls—*choron*—and shared with everyone present. After the kumys was drunk, there were games—horse races, wrestling, and archery.

A special set of kumys dishes, of which every family had a large supply, was brought out for the festival. The set included the choron bowls, wooden funnels, and carved buckets. The choron came in different sizes. The largest, from which kumys was drunk collectively, could be as tall as 80 centimeters and up to 90 centimeters in diameter at the widest part. Even the very largest goblets had a little base, which was incapable of supporting the bowl, especially when it was filled with kumys. This is evidence that the large *choron* were ritual bowls that were never meant to be set upright. They were handed around the circle until all the liquid was drunk and then turned over on the grass with the base upward *(Sel 'skomu uchitel' yu,* 1983:142). The choron was fashioned and decoratively carved from pieces of birch, using only an axe and a curved knife (the Yakuts did not have lathes). Often the choron was a tripod vessel with feet carved in the shape of horses' hooves. (Stylized horses' hooves were a common form in Yakut applied arts: tables stood on similar legs, and the funnel used to pour kumys resembled a horse's hoof (Potapov, 1972:90).) For the ritual libation, in addition to the choron, ladles for pouring the drink, funnels, whisks, leather sacks, birchbark pails, and small vessels were also used. The wooden parts of these objects were always decorated with horsehair, another way of emphasizing the important role of the horse in the culture of the Yakut people.

The unique utensils of the nomadic and seminomadic peoples were closely connected with their way of life and with traditions that took shape through their long history.

Harness
and Weaponry

Vadim P. Kurylëv, Larisa R. Pavlinskaya,

and Georgii N. Simakov

The horse harness, which today seems to us such a naturally integrated and simple apparatus, was not invented all at once. Several millennia passed before man, having tamed the horse, became a rider and invented the complete bridle and saddle complex used by equestrians today. The nomadic peoples of Eurasia played a key role in that evolutionary process.

The basic parts of the horse harness complex— the bridle, saddle, and stirrups—originated at different times. Thousands of years passed between the first appearance of the bridle, the most ancient element of the harness, and the final evolution of saddle with stirrups. The bridle gave people easy control over the horse, which had previously been hitched by a neck loop to a cart or a war chariot rather than ridden. The earliest remains of bridles date from the third millennium B.C. (Kovalevskaya, 1977:14) or even earlier. They consisted of a bronze bit with cheekpieces made of bone that connected the bit to straps around the horse's head. These remained the basic components of the bridle until the late Middle Ages. The oldest bridles have been found mostly in east Europe and are connected with the culture of the ancient Indo-Iranians (Kuz'mina, 1977:28–29).

The first evidence of the appearance of riders comes from the middle of the second millennium B.C. in a burial representing a late wood-felling (Russian: *srubnaya*) culture that covered the expanses of the steppes from the Dnepr to Kazakhstan (Smirnov, 1957:27). During the first millennium B.C., when nomadic animal husbandry arose on the Eurasian steppes and the horse became a basic source of mobility, there were corresponding innovations in equestrian equipment. The Scythian period saw the invention of the saddle, which permitted the rider to keep a firm seat on his steed, spend days, weeks, and even months on horseback, shoot arrows on the run, and handle a sword in close combat. The saddles consisted of two leather pillows sewn together and stuffed with grass or deerhair; they had soft leather arches reinforced with overlaid bone or wooden plates. Such saddles are well known to us from finds at the famous Pazyryk kurgans in the Altai. The saddle was fastened to the horse by a single girth-band with breast- and breech-straps. The ancient nomads had worked out the basic system for outfitting their riding horses. But these first saddles later underwent improvement.

The tradition of ornamenting harnesses originated in the same period. The most ancient decorative elements were made of animal bones or fangs (Gryaznov, 1980:47), but they were later replaced by overlaid plates and plaques of bronze and gold. These ornaments, fastened at the places where straps joined, prevented them from break-

Development of saddle and stirrup. 1. Egyptian warrior, fourteenth century B.C., Ramses II temple, Abu-Simbel. **2.** Assyrian warrior, seventh century B.C., Nineveh bas-relief. **3.** Scythian horseman-warrior, fourth century B.C., Kul'Obe kurgan; gold plaque (K-O 49), Hermitage, Leningrad. **4.** Horseman, fourth century A.D., clay figure found near Ch'ang-sha, central China. **5.** Wood-based saddle, fourth century A.D., near An-yang, China. **6.** Horseman, fifth or sixth century A.D., ceramic vessel, Silla Kingdom, Korea. **7.** Harnessed horse, seventh century A.D., ceramic figure, Japan. Figures 1, 2, and 4–7 after Vainshtein and Kryolov, 1985; their description of the development of the stirrup and saddle is summarized below.

An ancient Egyptian battle scene includes a warrior galloping on horseback (Figure 1). Although he holds reins, they are too long to control his steed; he is sitting in an awkward, unstable, and extremely uncomfortable position, almost on the horse's croup. Many researchers believe that the figure represents not an experienced rider but a deserter who has cut the traces of a chariot horse, clambered on, and fled from the field of battle.

In contrast, the Assyrian rider (Figure 2) sits on his horse in the way that we do today. He is galloping, having thrown down the reins to brandish his battle axe, and there is no doubt that he is a professional horseman. The Scythian (Figure 3) also rides with ease as he gallops into battle with his weapon raised.

At first glance the position of the rider from the fourth century A.D. (Figure 4) is no different from that of the Scythian—his legs hang free at the sides of his mount. But on the left side of his saddle there is a loop—a foot support used in mounting the horse—that is the prototype for the stirrup. A saddle found in a grave from the same period (Figure 5) had a rigid wooden base and vertical, flat arches, the forward arch somewhat smaller than the massive rear one. A gilded bronze "mounting stirrup" hung by a short strap from the left side of the saddle.

Many depictions of fifth and sixth century horsemen from the lower reaches of the Yangtze, the mountain valleys of Korea, and the Japanese islands have survived (Figures 6 and 7). They are all similar to one another and sharply different from depictions of riders in preceding epochs in that the mounted riders' feet are seated in stirrups. With feet in stirrups a rider has increased stability and ability to guide the horse.

1

2

PAGES 136, 140–141, top, 144–145
Detail of harness strap. From gear for a riding horse. Wood, leather, gold, velvet, metal. Early twentieth century, Yakuts. MAE 3687-12. Peter the Great's Museum of Anthropology and Ethnography, Leningrad.

An elaborate outfit for a horse was presented by the last Emir of Bukhara to the last Russian Emperor, Nicholas II.

PAGE 140 BOTTOM
Bride's saddle with stirrups. Wood, metal, leather Late nineteenth century, Yakuts. 55 centimeters long. MAE 334-11. Peter the Great's Museum of Anthropology and Ethnography, Leningrad.

ing and, in addition, served as talismans. In these ancient cultures a magic protective significance was attributed to the bones of animals, especially their fangs. Gold and bronze—metals that symbolized the sun and heavenly fire—had a similar significance (Ivanov, 1983:10). Depictions of animals that evidently embodied cosmic elements or represented deities protecting man and beast filled the same function.

The next stage in the development of harness for riding horses was the invention of a hard wooden saddle and stirrups. This was achieved by the nomadic peoples in the sixth century among the ancient Turks of central Asia and south Siberia (Vainshtein, 1966:65–67). The first hard saddles had low, sloping arches resting on two smoothly curved shelves. The separate pieces were joined by thin leather straps, which were passed through special apertures; this fastening system lent the entire structure a high degree of elasticity. Stirrups appeared soon after the hard wooden saddle. The first form of stirrup, a special wooden "step" attached to the left side of the saddle, was used not for riding but only as an aid in mounting (Vainshtein and Kryukov, 1984:123). It soon became clear that the stirrups were useful for riding, too. The hard saddle with stirrups then spread rapidly to other peoples. By the sixth century it was coming into use in ancient China and Korea.

The early Turkic saddles were the basis

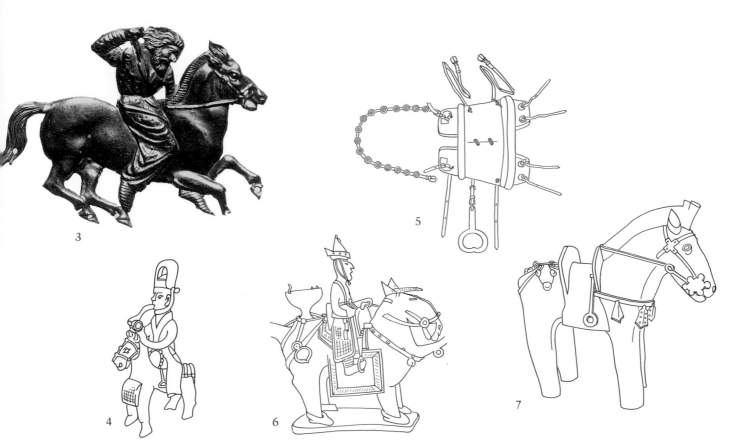

3

5

4

6

7

for new types that developed between the first and second millennia in various cultures of the steppes and were still characteristic of the nomadic herders of Eurasia up to the present century.

In Turkestan, Kazakhstan, south Siberia, and Mongolia in the nineteenth and early twentieth centuries there was only one type of riding harness, a good example of the sort of cultural phenomenon in which innovations of one people spread with astonishing rapidity. The harness became the property not only of all the herdsmen of the steppes but of most of the other peoples of the Old World as well. The harness consisted of a bridle and a saddle held to the horse by a girth-band and two straps keeping the saddle firmly in place against motions of the animal's croup and withers. Stirrups were fastened to both sides of the saddle, and straps with buckles could be used to change the stirrup's position to accommodate the size of the rider. These are the basic elements of our contemporary harness. But when we compare it to the equipment of the nineteenth-century herders of the Asian steppes, we see differences in external appearance and in the construction of individual items. The greatest variation is in the saddle.

The nineteenth-century saddles were massive wooden structures consisting of two planks called shelves with arches rising at either end. A quilted felt or leather pillow was fixed on

top of the shelves. These saddles were useful during long migrations and extended military campaigns. In this type of saddle, a rider could go limp or even doze off for a short time. Another distinguishing characteristic of the harness of the steppe-dwellers of one hundred years ago was the rich metal ornamentation that decorated all its elements. In most cases the saddle arches were covered with ornamental plates made of silver or iron inlaid with silver and sometimes even of gold. The saddle straps and bridle were decorated with a continuous row of metal plaques and plates, which were in turn covered with ornamental patterns. The role of metalwork artisans in decorating the nineteenth-century harness was a very active one. The overlaid plates, while following the shape of the various pieces of the harness, at the same time emphasized and exposed it.

Although there was a single way of constructing a harness, its separate elements took on specific forms characteristic of the historical development of the overall culture of one people or another. The greatest variety was observed in saddles and, more specifically, in the shape of the front arch. For example, the saddles of the Kazakhs and the Altaians had oval arches, and the same form was characteristic of the saddles of the Khakass and Yakuts as well. The arches of Tuvinian, Buryat, and Mongol saddles had a more triangular shape. The most unusual were the

Child's saddle with stirrups. Carved wood, metal. Early twentieth century, Kazakhs. Saddle 34 centimeters long. MAE 6852-26, 27. Peter the Great's Museum of Anthropology and Ethnography, Leningrad.

In the nomad world children were taught to ride from the age of six or seven, and sometimes even younger, with saddles and stirrups especially tailored to their size. The saddles had high arches to help the little rider keep a firm seat.

Opposite
Kirghiz riders. Early twentieth century. Photograph courtesy of Institute of Ethnography, Moscow and Leningrad.

saddles of the Kirghiz and Uzbeks, with front arches that looked like the long neck and head of a bird. In distinction to those of other peoples, the pieces of their saddles were not joined by straps but were instead glued together and covered with birchbark and a mesh made from animal sinews thickly smeared with glue as well. Instead of being ornamented in metal, these saddles were painted.

It is worth noting that many peoples had two, and sometimes three, different forms of saddle with varying shapes of the front arch. For instance, the Khakass and the Yakuts had saddles with nearly rectangular arches along with oval ones. The same saddles are seen among the trans-Baikal Buryats. Among the Khakass only women used these saddles. In general, however, there was no difference between nomadic men's and women's saddles. The women rode just as skillfully as the men.

The varying forms of saddle arch used by a single people is evidence of the complexity in the development of the nomadic culture of the steppe areas of Eurasia. The extraordinary mobility of the nomadic societies, the constant intermingling of different ethnic groups, and the occasional engulfing of one people by another led to heterogeneity in many elements of their cultures.

Fewer variations are observed in bridles and stirrups. These are almost identical every-

where, except among the Buryats, Mongols, and Tuvinians who had massive cast bronze stirrups, along with the iron stirrups common to all the area's peoples. The curved top of these stirrups near the aperture for the strap was often decorated with an animal head, usually a lion, dragon, or wolf. Many researchers see this as a survival of the Scytho-Siberian wild-animal style.

The nomads were masters of the skills of war and the entire repertory of martial strategems. Plano Carpini devoted a special section of his work to the Mongols' tactics. Among those developed over the centuries were painstaking observation of the enemy army, ability to choose the right moment to attack, raids to destroy lands far from the opponents' position, false flight aimed at luring the foe into a trap, and ways of making their own ranks appear larger than they actually were by putting women, adolescents, and even dummies on warhorses. The Mongols would storm well-fortified cities using ballistae and incendiary mixtures to set buildings afire and digging tunnels to undermine fortress walls or diverting rivers from their beds to destroy the walls in the flood.

A life passed in constant wars forced the nomad to keep his weapons close at hand. There is a curious scene on a breast ornament from Tolstaya Mogila in the Ukraine: two Scythians,

naked to the waist, are working over a ram's hide; although their activity is far from martial, a bow and several arrows lie beside them. The conviction in nomad society that each male was duty-bound to be a warrior survived until relatively recent times. According to Kazakh statutes—the "Steppe Codex" compiled by khan Tauke in the second half of the seventeenth or early eighteenth century—only the man who carried arms could be considered a full member of society (Levshin, 1832). Ancient legends attribute a martial character to the fair sex of the nomadic world as well. The image of the Amazons, popular in the art of ancient Greece, came from the steppe nomads who lived north of the Black Sea and the Caucasus. Herodotus thought that a people related to the Scythians, the Sauromatae, were the descendants of Amazons and Scythians. Among the Sauromatae, "no maiden may marry until she has killed a man of the enemy" (Herodotus 4.117, 1987:322). Contemporary archaeologists think that there is some truth in these legends: swords are frequently found in female burials ascribed to the Sauromatae or the Sarmatians. The image of the Amazons has been preserved to the present day in central Asian folklore—for example, in the Karakalpak epic, "Forty Maidens" ("Qïrq qïz").

The nomads could fight equally well in infantry formation or on horseback. But the nomadic warrior was above all a horseman skill-fully wielding his weapons. The choice of weapons changed relatively little up to the end of the Middle Ages. The Scythians' *chekan*—a battle axe with a very narrow "working" surface—was abandoned relatively quickly (evidently at the beginning of the Christian era); it was used to stab, rather than hack, and the term "axe" can be applied to it only with reservations. Simpler types of weapons—the cudgel, knife or dagger, and spear—remained unchanged for millennia. A Kazakh armed only with a strong cudgel would battle fearlessly against an enemy even in the late nineteenth and early twentieth centuries. The spear was widely used up to the beginning of the twentieth century. In the Middle Ages the Mongols used spears that had hooks in the neck, "and with this, if they can, they will drag a man from his saddle" (Plano Carpini, 1955:34.) Up to the early years of this century the Kirghiz practiced a military and sport competition called the "ër soyïsh," heroic combat with pikes. This was a form of chivalric tournament in which the object was to knock the opponent out of his saddle with a blow from a blunt pike while at full gallop. The spear usually served as a staff for the banner that inspired the warriors during battle. The pole-axe, which Herodotus mentions repeatedly in his account of the Scythians, was also still a dreaded war weapon among the peoples of Turkestan and Kazakhstan in the last century.

Saddle and saddle cover. Early twentieth century, Uzbeks. See page 138.

Boar's head battle axe. Bronze. Anan'ino burial, west of the Urals, seventh to third centuries B.C. 26.6 centimeter. MAE 1093-152. Peter the Great's Museum of Anthropology and Ethnography, Leningrad.

Depictions of a wild boar—a cautious, wily, and powerful beast who displays a terrible frenzy when aroused—are characteristic of the art of the early nomads. Boars' teeth were often used as amulets.

OPPOSITE

Battle axe. Steel, wood. Mid-nineteenth century, Kazakhs. 89.5 centimeters long. MAE 313-117. Peter the Great's Museum of Anthropology and Ethnography, Leningrad.

A dagger was concealed in the haft of this battle axe for use in case the warrior failed to fell his enemy with the axe. The battle axe was a popular weapon well into the late Middle Ages and was usually painstakingly ornamented. The axes of the Kazakhs, Kirghiz, and Uzbeks bore complex designs inlaid in silver. Sometimes their hafts were covered with leather and decorative plates. The tradition of decorating weapons can be traced back to early nomadic times.

The invention of the compound bow goes back to the most ancient times. The remains of such a bow were found in the Lake Baikal region in burials from the third millennium B.C. (Okladnikov, 1940). The design of the bow was evidently fully developed in Scythian times. The Scythians used a complex or compound bow glued together from several strips of wood; the central part was reinforced by plates made of horn or bone that gave the bow greater permanence, elasticity, and power. The small Scythian bow (0.6 to 0.8 meters long) was a powerful long-distance weapon. The ancient nomads could shoot their arrows accurately over their shoulders at targets behind them (the famous "Parthian shot") while they were riding at full gallop. Clement of Alexandria wrote that Sakian women "along with the men shoot backward as they pretend to flee." This tactic was used successfully by the nomads in the Middle Ages as well. As defensive armor began to spread in the early years of the Christian era, the Scythian bow was replaced by the so-called Hunnic bow, which was larger (1.2 to 1.6 meters long) and consequently had greater power and a longer range. On the march, the bowstring was unfastened at one end, and the bow itself kept in a special case, which along with the arrow quiver was fastened on a hook to the warrior's belt.

Arrows for the bow were made with various tips, depending on their intended use. Heavy metallic heads were needed to pierce enemy armor. A bone tip was used for war arrows. Ammianus Marcellinus (4th c.) wrote of the Huns: "They fight from a distance with missiles having sharp bone, instead of their usual points, joined to the shafts with wonderful skill." (Ammianus Marcellinus, XXXI, 2, 9). Hunting was done mainly with horn or bone arrowheads. Blunt arrowheads were used to kill fur-bearing animals to avoid damaging the skin. The shaft that protruded from the quiver was often decorated; different colors were used to denote each type of arrow, and the warrior could easily seize the one he needed.

Armor was widespread among the nomads by the Scythian-Sakian period. Archaeologists are familiar with the metallic helmets of the Scythians and Sakas, which resemble both the helmets of the Sumerians in the middle of the third millennium and those used in China from the thirteenth to the eleventh centuries B.C. In Scythian and Sakian burials hundreds of suits of armor have been found (Chernenko, 1968; Gorelik, 1987). Coats of mail were widely used by the nomads of the ancient Turkic period who followed an old military tradition of the steppes: to crush the enemy with an attack by heavily armed cavalry. The thick leather, which was used from ancient times as material for armor, did not lose its importance even in the Middle Ages. The Mongols, for example, made cuirasses from hides: "They take strips of ox-hide or of the skin of another animal, a hand's breadth wide, and cover three or four together with pitch, and they fasten them together with leather thongs or cord.... The upper part of the helmet is of iron or [copper]" (Plano Carpini, 1955:33–34). "These cuirasses...from multi-layered leather...are almost impenetrable...more permanent than iron" (Mansurova, 1979:150). The Mongols also covered their warhorses with armor. Shields were known to them, but they were never widely used.

Of course, not every warrior could manage to acquire the full set of weapons he needed. Minimal weaponry for the Mongol of the Middle Ages was as follows: "Two or three bows, or at least one good one, three large quivers full of arrows, an axe and ropes for hauling engines of war. As for the wealthy, they have swords pointed at the end but sharp only on one side and somewhat curved [sabers], and they have a horse with armour; their shins are also covered and they have helmets and cuirasses" (Plano Carpini, 1955:33). These observations by the thirteenth-century traveler are confirmed by ethnographic materials.

Sabers first appeared in the Eurasian steppes in the seventh and eighth centuries. "Many tribes took part in the creation of new weapons, first of all the Asiatic nomads as well as those struggling against them. The saber, intended as a light cavalry weapon, could originate only among warriors with room to maneuver" (Kirpichnikov, 1966:61). The saber is a more effective weapon from horseback than the sword. The curve of the blade and the tilt of the hilt give the saber a glancing blow that takes in a larger body surface. The saber was lighter than the sword and therefore could be wielded more rapidly. The evolution of the saber was evidently due to the invention of the hard saddle and stirrups that assured the rider stability on the horse's back and greater freedom to fight with cold steel.

Interestingly enough, the saber was slow to supplant the sword. To judge by archaeological finds, the nomads of the south Russian steppes were still using the sword in the thirteenth and fourteenth centuries. Even in the eighteenth and nineteenth centuries, however, not every Kazakh had a saber. The saber, like the spear and the battle axe, was treasured and passed down through the generations. In the northern Caucasus the sword disappeared only by the eighteenth century. The saber came to west Europe very late. On west European

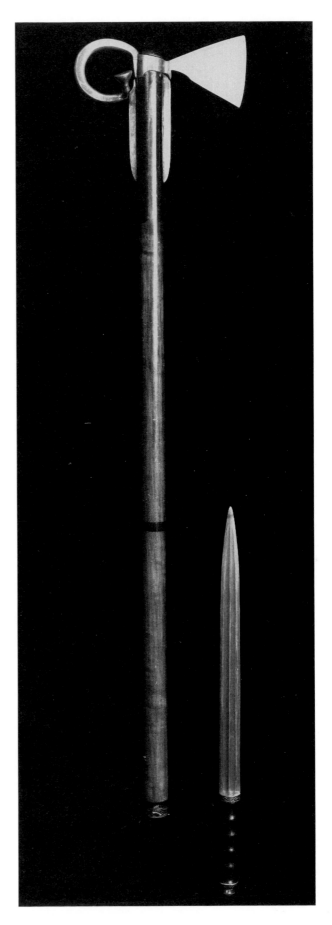

Helmet. Metal. Nineteenth century, Persians. 28 centimeters high. MAE 2872-1. Peter the Great's Museum of Anthropology and Ethnography, Leningrad.

OPPOSITE TOP
Round powder flask. Wood, leather. Late nineteenth century, Kazakhs. 17 centimeters in diameter. MAE 439-18. Peter the Great's Museum of Anthropology and Ethnography, Leningrad.

BOTTOM
Hood for bird of prey. Leather, fabric, metal. Early twentieth century, Uzbeks. 5 centimeters high. MAE 778. Peter the Great's Museum of Anthropology and Ethnography, Leningrad.

geographical maps dating from the sixteenth century, the depiction of Russian territory is accompanied by the figure of a "Moscovite" in a fur cap carrying a saber—in distinction to the European, who holds a sword. Sabers were accepted in medieval Europe as a symbol of Asia.

The lasso should also be mentioned among nomadic weaponry. Evidently it was not used at all times or by every group of nomads. However, the Huns used the lasso expertly in battles. Ammianus Marcellinus wrote that the Huns "fight hand to hand with swords, with no thought for themselves. When they become aware of the danger from enemy blades, however, they entangle [enemies] with sweeping throws of a lasso, so that, by drawing in the loop, they can take away their opponents' capability for moving on horseback or afoot" (Ammianus Marcellinus, XXXI, 2, 9).

Guns came rather late to the nomads of the Eurasian steppes—in the sixteenth and seventeenth centuries. Once they had been introduced to firearms, the nomads also began manufacturing them. Skilled smiths later made percussion-cap guns and even ones with fuses. These guns as a rule were massive and heavy and could be fired only from the ground, propped up on special bipods. Among all the weapons adapted to the horseman, the gun was therefore the only one that had to be used dismounted, and they were therefore relatively rare in nomadic circles. A Kazakh specialist of the mid-nineteenth century observed that "the gun, *multuk*, was a rarity on the steppes and passed from clan to clan and each one was given its own name…. It had a smooth barrel, a fuse, and little bipods made from saiga horns. They fired lead bullets. The Kirghiz [Kazakhs] as well as the Kalmyks and Bashkirs, made their own guns" (Valikhanov, 1985:37). The owner would always hang on his belt a bag containing a steel and flint and a spare fuse, a powder-flask, and also one or two little sacks of bullets.

The close connection of the nomadic way of life and the saddle horse led to original ways of hunting, an important factor in the economy of the nomads and seminomads and also their favorite sport.

From ancient times to the early twentieth century the nomads hunted by means of beaters and drives. They also used various kinds of traps and snares. Their basic weapon was the bow and, from the seventeenth century, the gun. Falconry was extremely widespread throughout

the steppes. Although the first mention of nomadic falconry dates from the Turkic epoch
(6th–7th cc.), hunting with birds of prey originated before nomadism itself; it was evidently
practiced in China in the second millennium
B.C. We have no direct evidence to confirm that
the Scythians and Sakas knew this form of hunting, but raptors were in use in the middle of the
first millennium B.C. in Japan and southwest
Asia, and the nomadic world must have known
it, too. It probably reached west Europe in the
first centuries A.D.

In the nineteenth and twentieth centuries hunting with raptors was particularly
popular among the Kazakhs, Kirghiz, Karakalpaks, and the seminomadic Uzbeks. The Turkmens also practiced it. Falcons, hawks, and also
eagles called *berkut* were used. Falcons and
hawks chased feathered game and rabbits; this
form of hunt was mainly for sport and recreation.
Berkut were loosed on foxes, marmots, and
young wolves for profit. The local traditions of
training birds of prey and their use are generally
like those of other regions where falconry is practiced. However, the large-scale character of the
hunt, the important place it occupied in the lives
of the peoples of Turkestan and Kazakhstan, and
their deferential attitude toward birds of prey

indicate that the hunt occupied a unique position among the nomads and that the area was one of the centers where falconry was born.

A captured bird of prey to be used in the hunt was deprived of sleep for several days to break its resistance and then was trained to sit on its master's arm and to accept its new environment; it was fed on chunks of meat washed free of blood in warm water, which it had to fly down and take from its master's hand. The last stage in training the bird was releasing it to attack dummies of game animals (roe deer, wolves, mountain goats, etc.); the bird was then tested in the field. The hoods, hobbles, and little bells used in handling birds of prey demonstrate the attention the hunters paid to the aesthetic aspects of their sport.

The peoples of the region were masters at handling raptors. It is enough to say that by the seventeenth century the Kazakhs were using falcons to hunt wild horses; even today the berkut is used in Kazakhstan to hunt wolves, wild boar, mountain goats, and even bears. Today only the Kazakhs, Kirghiz, and some Karakalpaks practice falconry in its traditional form; in the rest of Soviet Central Asia and Kazakhstan it has been completely supplanted by guns, traps, and snares.

Mirror. Bronze. Village of Taburishche, middle Dnepr region, fourteenth century, Mongols. 15 centimeters in diameter. GE 30.356. Hermitage, Leningrad.

This mirror is interesting in that it bears the scene of a falcon hunt. The Mongols practiced two forms of hunting: great battues organized by the aristocracy, which required the participation of large number of men, and the hunt for game by individuals. Hunting with raptors was the favorite method of going after game. Marco Polo gives an interesting description of a hunt organized by the Mongol ruler Khubilai-khan:

> Because he suffers from gout, the Great Khan always travels, when hawking, in a beautiful wooden shelter carried by four elephants. It is lined with beaten gold and the outside is covered with lion-skins. Kublai Khan always has twelve of his best gerfalcons with him and a number of barons and ladies to keep him company. As he travels along on top of the elephants his barons ride beside him drawing his attention to passing birds, such as cranes. The cover of the shelter is then thrown back and Kublai Khan sends out his best gerfalcons. They fight with the cranes for a long time and nearly always manage to capture them. Meanwhile the Great Khan lies back, delighting in the spectacle, with his barons and knights riding around him.

OPPOSITE LEFT
Kirghiz with hunting bird. 1950s. Photograph courtesy of Institute of Ethnography, Moscow and Leningrad.

RIGHT
A headless gravestone. Seventh or eighth century A.D., central Asia, Turks. Hermitage, Leningrad.

The figure holds a bird of prey, suggesting that the custom of hunting with birds was widespread among the Turks in the early Middle Ages.

Bowed Musical
Instruments

Vladimir N. Basilov

We know very little about the music of the ancient nomads. The semilegendary report of the Scythian ruler who refused to listen to the playing of a captured Greek prisoner, declaring that the finest music for him was the neighing of warhorses, does not reflect the early nomads' attitude toward music in general. The Scythians undoubtedly liked music and singing. For instance, a strange musical instrument, unlike any other of the time and called by archaeologists a "Scythian harp," was found during excavations in the Altai (the second Pazyryk kurgan) in the grave of a Scythian ruler who lived in the fifth century B.C. (Rudenko, 1953:324). The Scythians apparently wanted the dead man to enjoy music even in the other world. William of Rubruck, who traveled among the Mongols in the thirteenth century, saw "many...instruments such as are not known among us" (Rubruck, 1955:96).

The nomads shaped their own musical culture. We can get some idea of its distinctive features by studying peoples who retained the traditions of nomadic life into the nineteenth and twentieth centuries. Their music and singing were closely connected to oral poetry and especially to the ancient genre of the epos. Epic folk compositions glorifying the deeds of the heroes of old were usually sung to the accompaniment of musical instruments (although the Kirghiz bards called *manaschï* chanted the legends of the epic warrior Manas with no instrumental accompaniment). Music and poetry were inseparable from religious beliefs. The epic tales in particular were rich in mythological imagery; even their performance had the character of a rite. The nine-teenth-century Kirghiz manaschï Kel'dibek "was a healer, something like a shaman, who visited the sick, in particular women recovering from childbirth, and sang for them some episodes of 'Manas,' and this ritual had a curative property." The performance of "Manas" was also reputed to cure women of infertility. There is a legend that when Kel'dibek sang the tales of Manas, the wind rose, the earth shook, and cattle came running from the pasture to the yurts of their owners (Rakhmatullin, 1968:80).

The belief that a person received musical and poetic gifts at the will of the spirits was widespread. A Kirghiz became a bard, a manaschï, only after Manas himself or one of his fellow warriors appeared in a dream and

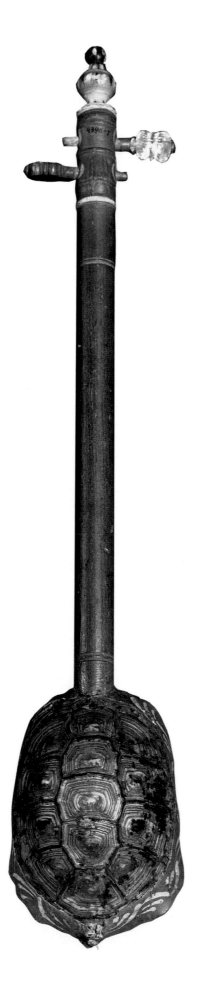

demanded that the man sing of their deeds. The talent of the famous Turkmenian poet Makhtumkuli (18th c.) came to him on the night when he received a blessing from the holy Muslim saints. Tutelary spirits in the shape of lions, tigers, wolves, ducks, and other animals appeared to the Kazakh folk singer-poet (aqïn), who also performed the epic. During poetry contests, if the aqïn saw his tutelary spirit at the moment of highest creative enthusiasm, he knew that he would win.

The beliefs of the nomadic and seminomadic peoples in the nineteenth and early twentieth centuries relating to music and poetry were close to shamanism. "The close resemblance between the legends of the calling of the singer and the tales of the calling of the shaman recorded among the same peoples are striking.... They undoubtedly reflect the same cultural tradition, since the profession of singer-bard and sorcerer-shaman at early stages of social development were connected" (Zhirmunskii, 1974:641–42). The shamans, when summoning their helping spirits, sang their incantations to music. Both the epic works and the shamanic invocations featured the same imagery and artistic devices. Many Uzbek and Kazakh shamans performed their incantations in an unnatural voice or screamed and whistled in the conviction that they were acting at the will of the spirits.

Apparently the nomadic and seminomadic peoples' faith in the supernatural origin of music and poetry was reinforced by the strange manner in which some of them per-

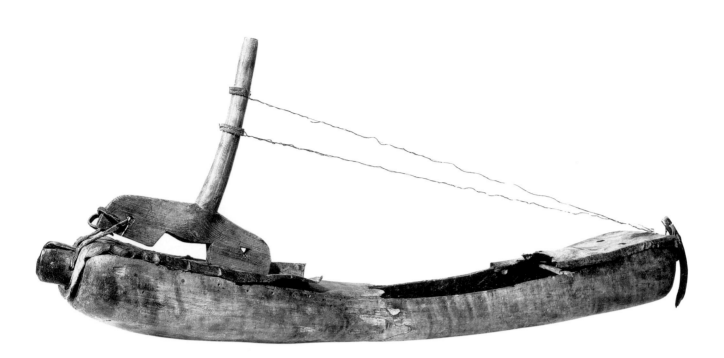

formed the epic works. The Altaian bards (*kaychï*) sang the heroic epos in a low hoarse voice. The Kazakh bard-singers (*jïrau*) usually performed the epic in a hoarse and tense voice. The rare phenomenon known as the "solo in two voices"—the singer produces two sounds, one high and the other low, simultaneously—was known only to Turkic and Mongol peoples. In the nineteenth and twentieth centuries this method of singing, which developed in the nomadic environment, existed among the Tuvinians, Buryats, Yakuts, and Bashkirs (Vainshtein, 1980). In the past the two-voiced solo was undoubtedly more widely disseminated and was probably perceived as a divine gift.

By the Middle Ages the musical instruments of the peoples who retained the traditions of nomadic life were varied. The nomads had wind, percussion, and stringed instruments. The mouth harp (or jaw harp), made out of metal (and, by the Tuvinians, Kazakhs, and Kirghiz, out of wood), was played everywhere. Bowed stringed instruments, noticeably different from European models, deserve special mention; they have much to tell us about the early history of the violin.

Today scholars of music seem united in the opinion that the first bowed instruments were created by the nomads and were borrowed by sedentary peoples. "Looking for the earliest evidences of the bow, we find the first mention in Persia in the ninth century; in China, a bowed zither is spoken of in the ninth or tenth century;

in Europe, fiddles are depicted in the tenth century.…Apparently the fiddle bow came to be known in the civilized world between 800 and 900 A.D." (Sachs, 1940:216). We may assume that bowed instruments reached sedentary peoples even earlier, but it would have taken some time for them to become widely used. Many authors believe that the fiddle came into Europe from the Arabs through Spain. Some medieval European fiddles are actually similar in form to the Arab *rebab*. However, there were more important paths of penetration. Europe received the fiddle both from Byzantium and directly from the nomads of the south Russian steppes. In its triumphal march it reached the farthest outposts of Eurasia, penetrating to the Indonesians, the Japanese, and the Chukchi. With each new people it took on a new appearance, without, however, always being improved. In east Europe in the nineteenth and early twentieth centuries singlestringed fiddles less complex than those of the nomadic peoples could still be seen. The wide variety of bowed string instruments in Asia, Africa, and medieval Europe leads to the conclusion that the European violin now in broad use throughout the world went through a long process of trial and error before it reached its contemporary shape.

What were the earliest forms of the violin? What did its ancient nomadic predecessors look like? Some evidence of the original construction of the instrument from which the violin evolved can be seen in the unusual Kazakh two-stringed bowed instrument, the *qïl qobïz* (the *kobyz* in western sources), and in the very similar Karakalpak *qobïz*, the Nogai *kobuz*, and the Kirghiz *kïyak (kïl kïyak)*. The kobyz is curved; the neck is constructed at an angle to the body of the instrument so that the strings lie at some distance from the body and the neck; the musician changes the sound by touching a finger (at the base of the nail) to a string. (This is similar to the method used in Indian and Mongol bowed instruments.) The kobyz did not change in design for many hundreds of years. This suggests that the neck of the proto-violin curved upward away from the body and the strings were at some distance from it. It was later, under the influence of plucked instruments, that the neck of the bowed instruments reached its modern position with the strings lying close to the surface of the finger-board to which they are pressed.

Part of the hollow body of the kobyz was covered with a skin membrane. The same type of membrane also partially or completely covers the body of the traditional bowed instruments of many Asiatic peoples (a soft membrane covering is not as characteristic, or is unknown, on plucked string instruments). Possibly the bowed instrument originated in connection with the discovery of the resonating quality of skin.

We do not know when the first bowed instruments appeared. The part of the sounding-board of the Kazakh kobyz covered with skin is similar in constuction to the corresponding part of the body of the Scythian harp of the fifth century B.C. The body of the Scythian harp is narrower through the midsection, and we assume that it was played with a bow. Of course there is no way that we can be sure that the instrument found in the Scythian grave was bowed. But the similarity in construction is evidence that the kobyz and related instruments represent a tradition that developed in the early nomadic environment.

Much clearer is the early connection of bowed musical instruments to religious practice in nomadic cultures. In European culture, this is not a characteristic role for the violin, which first appeared in Europe as a profane instrument used by common folk, often in accompaniment to clown shows. The opinion that it was a crude instrument is demonstrated by a drawing from the twelfth century: the upper half depicts King David with a plucked instrument in his hands while his musicians accompany him on wind instruments and bells; the lower half shows a mummer with acrobats beside him standing on their heads and turning somersaults to a tune

from a fiddle (Hughes, 1954). It did not take long for the fiddle to win high status in Europe, and a century or two later the angel playing a violin became a common image. The idea of the bowed instrument as a plebeian one was also common in India, and this is most likely explained by the comparatively recent foreign origin of bowed instruments.

In some nomadic cultures, on the other hand, the bowed instrument was clearly connected with the spirit world. Among the Kazakhs and Karakalpaks the kobyz had a ceremonial role; it was primarily the instrument of the shaman. To its sounds the shaman called his helping spirits. According to folk beliefs, the spirits themselves forced the shaman to pick up the kobyz. A Kazakh shaman (*baqsï*) told of spirits gathering one night in his yurt and announcing to him that he must become a baqsï. "Then my father's kobyz began to play all by itself and came toward me from the wall where it was lying. I picked it up and I haven't parted with it... for thirty years" (Alektorov, 1900:32). Another baqsï testified that to his surprise he began to play the kobyz only after he became a shaman. Some shamans forbade anyone to touch their instruments, threatening punishment from the spirits. Kazakhs and Karakalpaks believed that the kobyz was invented by the first shaman and singer, Korkut (a personage pre-Islamic in origin; with the establishment of Islam, Korkut became a Muslim saint, the protector of shamanism, poetry, and music). Metal pendants were fixed to the kobyz as to the Siberian shaman's drum; they made a noise whenever the baqsï shook his instrument sharply. The baqsï took good care of the kobyz, and it was passed from generation to generation. There are examples of kobyz in Soviet museums that have been repeatedly repaired, the cracked wood of the instruments having been carefully reinforced with iron bars at many places.

The Mongol-Buryat bowed instrument *khuur* also once had a ritual significance. It is often called the *morin khuur* (*morin* is Mongol for "steed"). Legend states that in ancient times the winged horse of a warrior was killed by an enemy. In memory of his beloved steed, the hero made a khuur from its skin, mane, and head, and the musical instrument became the embodiment of the winged steed. The rounded top of the neck of the khuur usually depicts a horse's head.

The occurrence of this sort of ornament is in my opinion not accidental. One finds similar engraved representations also on the handles

Kazakh *baqsï* or shaman. Early twentieth century.

The shaman's *qobïz* or *kobyz*, a traditional violin-type instrument, was made from a single piece of wood, and its strings were of horsehair. (The instrument is also called *nar-qobïz*. Since *nar* means "camel," the name suggests the ancient connection between the instrument and the camel; it is not by chance that Korkut, the first shaman and singer according to Kazakh legend, made the soundboard for the first kobyz from the hide of his camel.) Kazakhs thought that the kobyz had supernatural powers, because their shamans used it to accompany the songs with which they invoked their spirit helpers. The kobyz was played in a vertical or slightly inclined position; the instrument shown here is unusually large.

OPPOSITE
Kirghiz with kobyz. Early twentieth century.

PAGE 157
Khuur. Wood, leather, metal, horsehair. Early twentieth century, Mongols. 118 centimeters high. MAE 3495-4. Peter the Great's Museum of Anthropology and Ethnography, Leningrad.

The *khuur* or *morin-khuur*, a two-stringed bowed instrument that was widely used among the Mongols, was also known to the Buryats. The back section of the trapezoidal body is wood, the front is wood or leather. The neck is usually decorated with the jaws of a monster or dragon and topped with a horse's head, or sometimes three facing in different directions. Two horsehair strings are tuned to a fourth in the register of a small octave; the instrument is played in a vertical position.

of the staffs used by the Mongol shamans in the performance of their rites. This agreement seems to indicate that the Mongol fiddles were at one time shaman instruments, and originally, in the same way as the shaman staffs and the shaman drums, represented the mythical riding animals upon which, as the Mongols imagine, the shamans rise on their journeys into the realm of spirits (Emsheimer, 1943:85).

Survivals of the shaman's magic riding animal are retained in popular beliefs about the kobyz. According to Kazakh legend, a powerful baqsï put his kobyz to race against horses; of course, the kobyz, flying through the air, came in first against the fastest steeds.

The origin of the violin is therefore intimately connected with the ancient shamanic beliefs of the nomadic peoples.

Religious
Beliefs

Vladimir N. Basilov and Natal'ya L. Zhukovskaya

Like most other ancient peoples, the early nomads believed in multiple gods who ruled over nature and humans; Herodotus had no difficulty in finding equivalents of the Scythian gods in the Greek pantheon. Evidence of the similarity between the religious outlook of the Scythians and Sakas and those of the ancient Iranians and Aryans who conquered India in the second millenium B.C. gives us reason to assume that the ideology of the peoples of the Scytho-Sakian culture was no less sophisticated and complex.

Religious thought continued to evolve among the nomadic peoples, and by the Middle Ages, the concept of a powerful supreme god was clearly established on the Eurasian steppes. Ibn-Faḍlān, who traveled in the tenth century through the lands of the Turkic Oghuz, heard them appealing to a single high god called Tengri. William of Rubruck (13th c.) was granted an interview with the Mongol sovereign Möngke-khan and recorded his words: " 'We Mongols,' said he, 'believe that there is but one God, by Whom we live and by Whom we die' " (Rubruck, 1955:195).

But this continuing independent development of religious beliefs in the nomadic environment was interrupted in the Middle Ages by the spread of the so-called major religions. The proselytizing success of these religions was due above all to the political power behind them. By accepting one of them, the nomadic peoples in essence were defining their place among the powerful medieval states.

Despite the intrusion of Buddhism, Christianity, and Islam some of the original religious beliefs of the nomadic and seminomadic peoples persisted. One of the most interesting of these survivals was shamanism. It was preserved into the nineteenth and twentieth centuries in its most impressive form among the Altaians, Khakass, Tuvinians, Yakuts, and Buryats.

Shamanism is one of the most ancient types of religious cult. It is based on a belief that certain people (shamans) can serve as intermediaries between humans and spirits (deities). It was thought that shamans could make contact with the spirits, learn their will, and inform their fellow tribespeople of the sacrifices the spirits wished them to make. The shaman's basic functions included healing diseases (which were believed to be caused by the spirits), divination, prophecy, and tracking down missing objects and

PAGE 160 AND RIGHT
Shaman's caftan. Fabric, fur, metal. Nineteenth century, Altaians. 169 centimeters long. MAE 5064-2. Peter the Great's Museum of Anthropology and Ethnography, Leningrad.

Altaian shamans, both men and women, provided themselves with ceremonial garments only after they had had a dream in which the costume was described to them in detail by their tutelary spirit, who indicated the number, shape, and size of the pendants it should bear. Sewing the costume was the prerogative of the women of the shaman's family; they were helped by those from neighboring yurts and supervised by an elderly woman well acquainted with local customs. When the costume was finished, the shaman carried out a rite during which the patron spirit was to examine the costume to make certain that his specifications were met. If he did not approve it, the work would have to be done over.

The costume was made of sheep- or deerskin and covered with various pendants. Depictions of helping spirits occupied an important place; for example, small dots representing the daughters of the supreme god Ülgen, the sky-dweller, who would aid the shaman in ascending to the upper world were sewn to the back of the collar. A belt with a dense braided fringe representing snakes was sewn to the cloak. Obligatory appurtenances of the cloak were two plaques symbolizing the sun and moon. Throughout his life the shaman would add pendants as he grew in experience and acquired new spirit helpers.

OPPOSITE LEFT
Shaman's "crown." Metal. Nineteenth century, Buryats. 20.5 centimeters in diameter. MAE 2016-36. Peter the Great's Museum of Anthropology and Ethnography, Leningrad.

Among some peoples of Siberia the shaman wore an iron headdress, given to him only after he had proved to his fellow tribespeople that he and his spirit helpers could be beneficial to them.

Each element of the ceremonial costume of the shaman had great significance, and he had to wear the costume to transform himself into or associate freely with the spirits, which were often imagined as taking the shape of animals. One mark of faith in the shaman's ability to turn into animal and bird spirits was the shape of his cloak: among a number of peoples it was longer in back, and in it the shaman resembled a bird with a tail. The shaman's headdress also had features reminiscent of animals or birds. This crownlike iron cap is decorated with a depiction of antlers as an indication of the shaman's connection with the upper world (the deer was long perceived as an animal connected with the heavenly sphere).

RIGHT
Shaman's horse sticks. Wood, metal. Nineteenth century, Buryats. 104 centimeters long. MAE 1109-3/2. Peter the Great's Museum of Anthropology and Ethnography, Leningrad.

In the nineteenth century, most Buryat shamans used the horse stick or cane as their chief ceremonial object. The horsehead finials of these canes were symbolic of the steed that carried the shaman into far countries and other worlds. Each Buryat shaman used two horse sticks in his rites, and the sticks of important shaman were made of iron.

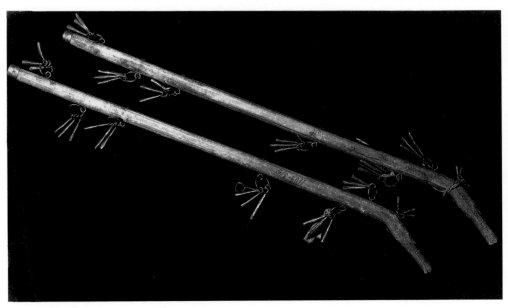

animals. Among some Siberian peoples the shamans had a duty to assure an abundance of wild animals and successful hunting and fishing, to chase wolves away from the common herds, and to protect their fellow tribespeople from misfortune and sickness. The power to produce changes in nature (to call forth bad weather or rain) was also ascribed to the shamans. All this the shamans were to carry out with the aid of their guardian or helping spirits.

Women as well as men could become shamans. Among many peoples (for example, the Buryats) there are legends that women were the first shamans. The social position of the shamans varied—some were dreaded and reverenced, others were treated with no special deference. It depended on both the place of shamanism in the religion of the particular people and the shaman's personal qualities. All peoples everywhere feared a "strong shaman" and cajoled him with gifts.

Shamanism was considered a family trait and a person was supposed to follow in the steps of his shaman ancestors. But it was thought that the spirits themselves chose the person who became a shaman. The future shaman saw in trances or dreams spirits who proposed that he become a shaman. The outward sign that he had been chosen was an excruciating illness—the chosen person fell into delirium, committed strange acts, and sometimes behaved violently or

disappeared for a time. The illness was taken by those around him as a temporary eclipse of his reason, a sign that he was in the power of spirits who had carried him off invisibly to the other world to teach him the shaman's art. There he underwent the most refined tortures: the spirits cut off his limbs, killed him, hacked him apart; then he was "reconstituted," brought back to life, and released. The chosen one who submitted to this process was considered newly born after his time in the spirits' hands and was freed of his illness. But if he refused to obey the spirits' demands, his sufferings were aggravated, and dreadful mutilation and ostensibly even death could ensue.

The shaman usually communicated with the spirits during rituals when, to the sound of the drum or some other musical instrument, he called on his helping spirit and, lapsing into an ecstatic state, portrayed his voyage to other worlds. If a fellow tribesman's illness was caused by spirits of the underworld, the shaman went there to abduct or ransom the sick person's soul from the spirits who had stolen it. Among the Altaians and other peoples, the shaman accompanied the soul of a dead person into the underworld. If illness or economic indigence demanded a trip to heaven—to the spirits or deities of the "upper" world—the shaman depicted his flight there. His ecstatic state meant that the spirits had taken possession of the shaman. The

Shaman's drum. Leather, wood, metal. Nineteenth century, Altaians. 63 centimeters in diameter. MAE 5064-10. Peter the Great's Museum of Anthropology and Ethnography, Leningrad.

The tree used to make the rim of a shaman's drum (*tonur* or *chalu*) was chosen in accordance with the instructions of the shaman's tutelary spirit; it was generally a clean, unscarred birch or cedar that grew at some distance from human habitation. The hide of a deer or young horse was stretched over the rim of the drum. The drum handle, which was shaped like a human figure, depicted the spirit of the "master" of the drum, the ancestral shaman; pendants on either side of the head of this figure represented the ancestor's ears and earrings. The iron bar at breast level on the handle represented both the ancestor's arms and a bowstring. Arrow-shaped iron pendants hung from the bowstring, and during the rites the shaman would mime using these arrows to strike down evil spirits and his competitors, hostile shamans. Before and after the rites his fellow tribespeople would hang cloth ribbons on the crosspiece of the drum as offerings to the spirits.

The drum's outer and inner surfaces were painted with red and white paints from natural substances. There were no specific subjects prescribed, but the paintings usually included depictions of heavenly bodies, deities or spirits, the ancestor-shaman, and sacred trees and animals. On this drum, for instance, the starry sky is indicated by circles, and the ten little figures sitting on the bowstring-crosspiece of the drum are the ten daughters of the Altaian supreme god Ülgen. Traditionally the Altaians understood the drum to be a living creature (a horse) on which the shaman in ecstasy made his voyages into other lands, the skies, and the spheres of the underworld.

After a drum was made, a special rite had to be performed to bring it to life. The Altaians believed that during his lifetime the shaman would use the exact number of drums—three, five, or nine—prescribed by his patron spirit. The shaman used each drum for some years, and when the period of the last drum ran out, the shaman died. His drum, with holes in it to show that it was also dead, was hung on a tree not far from the place where the shaman was buried.

Shaman's tutelary spirit. Wood. Early twentieth century, Yakuts. 15 centimeters long. MAE 4774-7. Peter the Great's Museum of Anthropology and Ethnography, Leningrad.

The shaman received his strength and supernatural powers from the spirits. Many peoples distinguished one powerful guardian or tutelary spirit among a shaman's spirit helpers. In some cultures (for instance, among the Buryats) this spirit was thought to be the ancestor-shaman, and it took the form of an animal. According to Yakut beliefs, the shaman was magically connected with an animal guardian spirit called the "mother-beast"; when the beast perished, the shaman died. At the same time the Yakut shaman also imagined his patron spirit *(emeget)* in human form, and he bore that human image on the most prominent metal pendant of his costume, usually affixed to the back of his collar.

Although not intended to be used on a costume, this little figure of a guardian spirit riding a bird was made for shamanic rituals.

ABOVE
Shaman's mask. Metal. Nineteenth century, Buryats. 23 centimeters high. MAE 2016-45. Peter the Great's Museum of Anthropology and Ethnography, Leningrad.

LEFT
Drumstick. Bone, deerhide. Late nineteenth century, Yakuts. 36 centimeters long. MAE 4128-447. Peter the Great's Museum of Anthropology and Ethnography, Leningrad.

The drumsticks of Yakut shamans were usually made of wood or elk or deer antlers carved into a narrow, slightly curved scoop with a short handle. A piece of hide with the hair side up was stretched over the convex striking surface of the stick. The handle was sometimes carved in the shape of a beast's head. For the Yakuts and a number of other peoples, the drum was a symbol of the horse that the shaman rode on his journeys, and therefore the drumstick was his whip.

Uzbek shamanic ceremony.
Dzhizakskaya oblast, 1979. Photographs by V. N. Basilov.

In this annual or semiannual ritual of "getting of blessing" or "renewal of blessing" (*pataa alish* or *pataa jangalash*), a shaman seeks to contact her spirit helpers with the aid of another older or more experienced shaman; relatives of the shaman who participate also receive the benediction of the shaman's helping spirits.

At the beginning of the ceremony (top), the group prays (note that they hold their hands in the traditional Muslim way). The ritual food has been eaten, and the bones of the sacrificial ram as well as water, bread, and candles have been placed on a cloth in front of the two shamans. As the ceremony progresses, the shamans—and then the sister of the woman to be blessed (bottom)—fall into a trancelike state of ecstasy.

Opposite
Teleut woman shaman. 1930s.
From Dyrenkova, 1949:108.

The pictures on the shaman's drum, which reflect traditional folk beliefs, are divided into two parts that together symbolize the earth. Among the figures in the large upper area is a red square with two zigzagging lines in it called "the handwriting of White Ülgen"; without this document from the supreme god Ülgen, the shaman cannot begin to serve. The white square represents a net with which, at the shaman's order, seven of the birds depicted on the drum will try to catch the soul of a sick person if it escapes or is carried off by spirits. The guardian spirit of the shaman is depicted in human shape, holding a saber. Among the drawings on the lower part of the drum are several of the shaman's spirit helpers, including a fish and a frog who accompany her on her dangerous journeys to the spirits.

Drum. Leather, wood, metal. Nineteenth century, Shors. 56 centimeters in diameter. MAE 5073-3. Peter the Great's Museum of Anthropology and Ethnography, Leningrad.

Like many other peoples, the Altaians, Khakass, Shors, Buryats, and Tuvinians conceived of the universe as divided into three worlds. Deities and spirits dwelt in the upper sky world, and people resided in the middle world; the lower world was the gloomy realm in which human souls ended up after death. The drawings on the drum, the shaman's main ceremonial instrument, reflect these concepts of the universe and also the shaman's ideas of his calling. This drum bears depictions of sky spirits: we can make out misshapen creatures with three fingers and chicken feet, and among them the shaman himself on a horse, carrying his drum and drumstick. This evidently signifies that the shaman was chosen by the skyworld spirits; it is not by chance that the drawing is in red paint (sky spirits were usually depicted in red, and underworld ones in black).

OPPOSITE
Khakass horse consecration. Abakan River basin, 1914. Photograph courtesy of Peter the Great's Museum of Anthropology and Ethnography, Leningrad.

The shaman, with his drum, leads the ceremonial procession around a birch tree; after the horse tied to the tree has been anointed with milk, its mane will be decorated with fabric and it will be released to run free.

The Khakass were considered converted to Christianity by the beginning of the twentieth century. Thus the participants in this pagan religious ceremony were most likely Orthodox Christians.

shaman in ecstasy might fall unconscious, imitate animal sounds and actions, manifest heightened sensitivity or, on the contrary, fail to feel pain from a knife or fire. He was completely under the spell of his visions.

As late as the mid-twentieth century there was a widely accepted scientific opinion that shamans were psychotics suffering from a nervous disorder; shamanism was even called a "cult of madness" (Ksenofontov, 1929). But the facts do not confirm this appraisal. An experienced shaman could regulate his condition and fall quickly into ecstasy; some fasted or used narcotics before beginning the ceremony to heighten sensitivity to the spirits. But all had a profound belief in their appeals to spirits, in the truth of their visions, and in the reality of their journeys to other worlds. Their sincere faith in the spirits explains the nature of the shamanic illness and his states of ecstasy. The unusual behavior of the shaman during his illness and ritual ecstasy was expected, reinforced by the traditional culture (Basilov, 1984:139–169).

The rituals demanded great physical endurance from the shamans; making predictions or finding lost articles demanded unusual powers of observation or intuition. The shamans not only carried out the functions of priest, magician, and healer, but they were also musicians, singers, and poets. During the ceremonies they did things of which ordinary people

were not capable. Some shamans among the Yakuts, Buryats, and Kirghiz showed those present that they could cut off their own heads or those of their patients and then restore them to place and cause them to adhere. The ritual was a dramatic event that produced a deep impression on those present. Only people of exceptional inspiration and talent could successfully practice the shaman's profession.

Information about shamans collected in the nineteenth and twentieth centuries gives us some conception of the beliefs of the early nomads, for whom the shaman occupied an important social position, as well as information on the behavior and fates of certain later shamans. It is true that a Scythian ruler had soothsayers and their sons put to death if their prophecies failed (Herodotus). But a later Chinese source relates the story of the court shaman to Cheunu, ruler of a powerful central Asian tribe called the Jou-jan. The khan "greatly respected and loved her and, following her advice, made a muddle of governing." The female shaman's intrigues created confusion at Cheunu's headquarters, and in 520 she was killed, and the ruler afterwards as well (Bichurin, 1950:197). In the tenth century an anonymous author wrote that the Turkic Oghuz honored their healers (evidently, shamans): "these healers ordered their life and their property" (Ḥudūd al-'Alam, 1937:100). The Mongol shaman Teb-

tenggeri promoted the rise of Chingis-khan by confirming that the gods had chosen Chingis sovereign over the world. Teb-tenggeri was an important figure at Chingis-khan's headquarters but was finally killed when his constant meddling irritated the ruler (Rashid ad-Din, 1952:167–168; Grousset, 1967:176–181). But shamans did not remain out of favor long. A large group of them, headed by a powerful leader, lived at the headquarters of Mïngke-khan, Chingis-khan's grandson; these shamans were feared because they could condemn an innocent person by accusing him of witchcraft (Rubruck, 1955:197–201).

With the establishment of the major religions, shamanism lost its previous social significance and became an unofficial and marginal cult. Buddhism and Christianity penetrated into central Asia and east Turkestan in the early centuries A.D. even before the Arab conquests. "The caravan route went from the Mediterranean to the Yellow Sea. Along it, across deserts and mountains, streamed ideas, systems, and beliefs along with silks and attars" (Gumilev, 1967:77).

Beginning in the seventh century, after the incursion of Arabian warriors, Islam was propagated energetically in central Asia and east Turkestan. The dissemination of the Muslim religion, however, took several centuries. Even after the partitioning of Chingis-khan's empire,

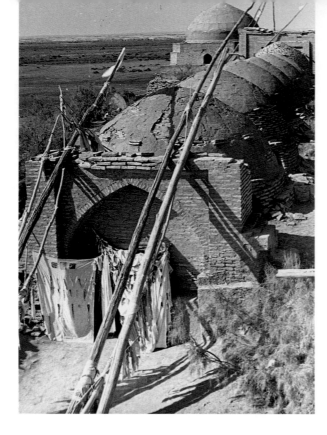

Muslim saint's tomb. Khorezm oasis, Tashauz oblast, Turkmen S.S.R., 1980s. Photograph by V. N. Basilov.

The religious centers of the central Asian oases have always attracted the people of the steppes. When Islam became important in this region, its holy places came to be venerated by the nomads. Especially popular were the tombs of the Muslim saints that, like this one, were on the boundaries between the cultivated lands and the desert.

Pilgrimages are made to this tomb, that of Saint Ismamut-ata, who according to Turkmenian legend lived at the time of the Prophet Muhammed.

RIGHT
Dervish's cap. Satin, cloth. Late nineteenth century, Uzbeks. 27 centimeters high. MAE 1487-4. Peter the Great's Museum of Anthropology and Ethnography, Leningrad.

OPPOSITE
Muslim dervishes. Bukhara, early twentieth century. Photograph by S. Dudin, courtesy of Peter the Great's Museum of Anthropology and Ethnography, Leningrad.

Roaming dervishes, fanatic representatives of the mystical Sufi trend in Islam, were encountered everywhere in Muslim countries. As a sign of their renunciation of worldly things, the dervishes had no profession and lived on alms; some of them did not marry. They appeared in the bazaars and on city and village streets, in groups or singly, chanting religious verses; their rules forbade begging, but they received alms because people believed that it was bad luck not to give them food or money (Sukhareva, 1960).

Dervishes belonged to various Sufi orders that differed in details of beliefs, practices, and dress. The shape of the cap of a Qalandar dervish can be traced back to the headdresses worn by early nomads, and it is possible that the geometric patterns embroidered on it are an imitation of ancient ornamentation.

"in all the Mongol domains there was a struggle among Christians, Buddhists, and Muslims, all of whom were endlessly striving to win over the khans" (Bartol'd, 1964:263). Some Mongol khans, influenced by their Christian and Buddhist advisors, issued edicts against the Muslims. But the political situation developed in favor of Islam. By the tenth century Islam had taken hold in the oases of Turkestan, and by the sixteenth century it was firmly established among the nomads, including the Kazakhs and Kirghiz, who had held onto their pagan religion longer than the other peoples of the region.

By the nineteenth century the only relic of Christianity was the cross-shaped brand *(tamga)* of one of the Kazakh tribes (K-v, 1903). Islam had triumphed over the vast territories of the herders' primordial migrations: Middle Asia and Kazakhstan, the southern part of west Siberia, the northern Caucasus and parts of the Transcaucasus, the lower Volga, and the western foothills of the Urals.

Buddhism and Christianity were very late in establishing a foothold in the life of a number of herding peoples. At the end of the sixteenth century Lamaism (one of the branches of Buddhism) began to spread through Mongolia, where it was accepted as the state religion by the middle of the seventeenth century. In the early seventeenth century Lamaism reached Tuva (without, however, winning over all groups of Tuvinians), and from the end of the eighteenth century it was to be found in Buryatia (princi-

pally among the eastern Buryats).

Orthodox Christianity began to be propagated late in the seventeenth century after Siberia was annexed to the Russian Empire. It took hold among the seminomadic western Buryats and Yakuts. "Russian Orthodox missionaries were active in the Altai from the 1820s, but the results of that activity varied widely from region to region" (Tokarev, 1958:441). The Khakass and the northern Altaians were almost all converted to Orthodoxy; but the polytheistic religion of the southern Altaians, who were still leading nomadic and seminomadic lives, continued to exist along with Christianity.

The tenets of Christianity and Buddhism are so well known that we need not characterize them further. But Lamaism is less familiar and therefore needs describing. Lamaism is among the most recent sectarian movements in Buddhism. Its homeland is Tibet, where the earliest schools of Lamaism took shape from the eighth to the eleventh centuries. In ideology and practice these schools are tightly intertwined with the mythology of ancient India, the philosophical concepts of the Vajrayāna—the most esoteric of the Buddhist doctrines—and, finally, the traditional beliefs and rites of Tibet itself. In European literature this new movement was called "Lamaism" from the Tibetan word "lama" ["the highest one"], the title of the teacher-mentor in the monastery schools of Tibet. The Tibetans themselves called the religion of Buddha "the

way" or "the law," and each order of Lamaism had its own designation, namely *bKa 'gdams pa [bKa 'brgyud pa], Sa skya pa, rNying ma pa,* and *dGe lugs pa.* The dGe lugs pa order, which was founded at the beginning of the fifteenth century by the most important reformer of Tibetan Buddhism, Tsong kha pa, quickly occupied a leading position in Tibet and later penetrated into Mongolia, Buryatia and Tuva.

Like all Buddhists, the Lamaists worship Buddha as a teacher who shows the world the way to deliverance from suffering. They believe that all beings live in the phenomenological world of *saṁsāra,* where they are doomed to be reborn an endless number of times. Rebirth in a new aspect is regulated by the law of *karma*—retribution for sins committed in earlier incarnations. It is only by entering upon the path of Buddha and discovering the truth within themselves that humans can begin the ascent along the path to salvation. The goal of existence for every living thing in the universe is *nirvāṇa,* a final extinction of the consciousness, where the soul is completely freed from earthly attachments and earthly guises. This goal can be reached by every believer who chooses the right path.

There are several characteristics of Buddhism that are specific to Lamaism. In Lamaism a cult of personal guardian-deities for each believer developed; the concept of the spiritual teacher took on unusual dimensions in that the teacher-mentor guided his disciple's every

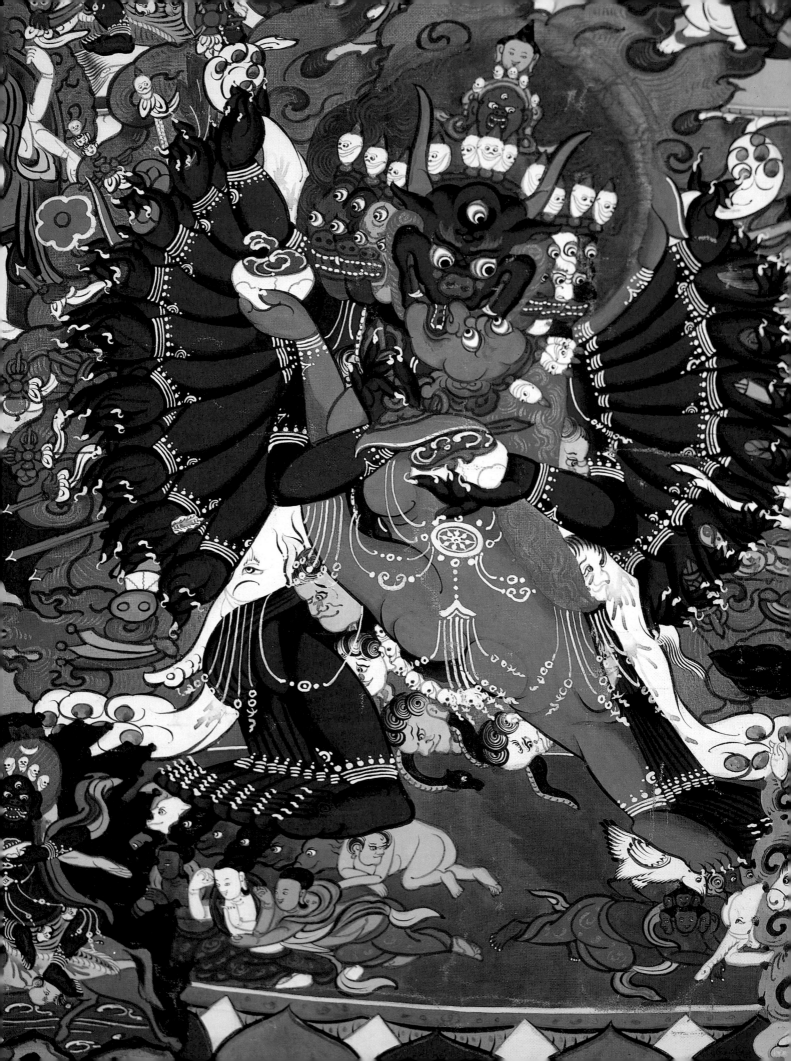

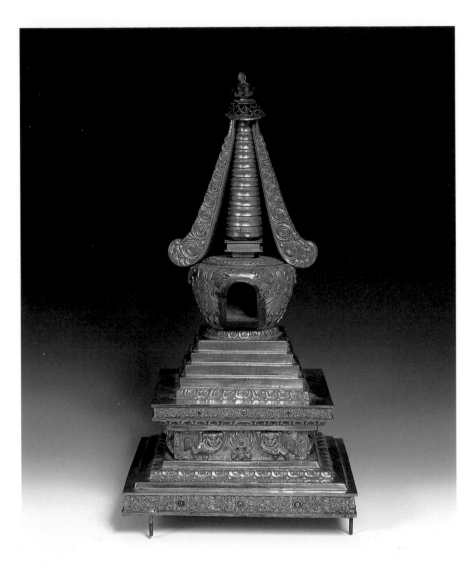

OPPOSITE

Icon. Fabric. Nineteenth century, Buryats. 118 centimeters long. MAE 187-7. Peter the Great's Museum of Anthropology and Ethnography, Leningrad.

Icons painted on fabric are characteristic of Lamaism. They depict deities or groups of deities, as well as compositions explaining philosophical concepts of Buddhism.

    This icon shows Yamandaga (Sanskrit: Yamāntaka), the conqueror of the god of death, Yama. He is portrayed as wrathful, signifying his ability to destroy apathy and negative emotion.

    In Buryat temples a depiction of Yamandaga is included in the iconostasis of the altar, and pious Buryats keep his image in their homes as a protective deity. The Mongols and Buryats identified Yamandaga with the Turkic god Erlik, the master of the underworld and supreme judge in the world beyond the grave.

Suburgan. Bronze. Nineteenth century, Buryats. 37 centimeters high. MAE 4698-482. Peter the Great's Museum of Anthropology and Ethnography, Leningrad.

In the Buddhist canon the suburgan, a form of stūpa, had a double role: as a memorial monument and as a repository for holy relics. In Buryatia, Tuva, and Mongolia it was used in the same way as the Indian stūpas although it differed from them in shape.

    In temple architecture suburgans were complex and monumental towerlike structures with three basic parts: pedestal, central main section, and spire. The religious architecture of the central Asian peoples included eight types of suburgan (the suburgan of advocacy, the suburgan of death, the suburgan honoring the spread of Buddhism, etc.). The temple of Erdene-Zuu in Mongolia is surrounded by a stone wall of 108 suburgans.

    Miniature suburgans copied one type or another of the canonical stūpas and were used for altars in temples and houses. Prayer texts or depictions of Buddha or saints of the Lamaist pantheon were often placed inside the miniature suburgans. In meditation the stūpa was seen as a vertical model of the universe that could be gradually reproduced in the meditator's consciousness to facilitate the process of fusion with the universe.

Opposite and Above
Ivolginsk Lamaist monastery. Buryat A.S.S.R., 1984.
Photographs by O. Makarov.

action, thus reducing the student's initiative in the search for truth to a minimum. It was only in Lamaism that the cult of "living buddhas"—people who were considered to be earthly incarnations of the leading gods of the Buddhist pantheon or of heroes of Buddhist history—originated and was generally accepted. The best known of the living gods are the Dalai-lama (the incarnation of the Bodhisattva of Mercy or Aralokiteshvara) and Mañjuśrī, the Panchen-lama (the incarnation of the Buddha of Infinite Light, Amitabha).

Specific to Lamaism are special forms of indoctrination, through which, for example, adepts are able to call down the "internal fire" within themselves and to delay their death to a designated day and hour. In the mythology of Lamaism the concept of Shambhala, the land of universal physical and spiritual prosperity, was particularly highly developed.

Lamaism everywhere superimposed itself on preexisting cults and beliefs. Initial unsuccessful attempts to extirpate pagan traditions by force were replaced by political development of neutral or syncretic norms for the rites; manuscript descriptions of "shamanic" practices evolved into handbooks for Lamaist ceremonies honoring local gods and saints. In these, almost all the major shamanic spirits or local deities had a page added to their mythological biography in which it was related how, when, and why the de-

ity became Buddhist and who helped it to enlightenment (this was most often an encounter with Buddha or the Dalai-lama). The spirit's current role in Buddhism was also described. The most popular shamanic deity of the Mongols, Buryats, and Kalmyks, Chagan Ebügen (White Old Man), the guardian of longevity, wealth, and fertility, was brought into the local Buddhist pantheon: his iconography and biography told how Buddha, out walking with disciples, met a white-bearded, noble-looking elder, struck up a conversation with him, and became convinced of his wisdom. Chagan Ebügen was then declared a Buddhist saint.

The mythology, ritual practices, and sacred objects of Lamaism on the Eurasian steppes show the influence of a shamanism that goes back to the earliest currents of human thought. It is easy to see a resemblance between the masks and costumes of the characters portrayed in the central Lamaist festival *cham* and the masks and costumes of the shamans of Siberian and central Asian peoples, and in the depictions on ancient petroglyphs (dancing figures in horned headdresses). Many decorative motifs and symbols, which we now think of as Buddhist (the lotus, the endless thread of fortune, the

Drum. Wood, leather. Nineteenth century, Mongols. 50 centimeters in diameter. MAE 719-84. Peter the Great's Museum of Anthropology and Ethnography, Leningrad.

Lamas used the drum during temple services and rites performed outside the temple in pauses between different prayers.

BOTTOM

Musical instrument. Conch, metal. Nineteenth century, Buryats. 21 centimeters long. MAE 4698-167. Peter the Great's Museum of Anthropology and Ethnography, Leningrad.

The conch *Strombus*, which is highly valued for its white color and clockwise spiral, is used as a musical instrument during services in Buddhist monasteries. The Indian tradition places it among the regalia of imperial power as a symbol of enlightenment, and in Buddhism it came to represent the voice of the preaching Buddha. The shell is among the "eight emblems of glory," eight objects that play an important role in rituals; it is one of the signs imprinted in Buddha's footsteps. The conch is used as a musical instrument outside the Buddhist world as well: small boats that fish the coastal waters of east and southeast Asia use it as a foghorn.

OPPOSITE TOP

Sheep scapula. Nineteenth century, Buryats. 15 by 11 centimeters. MAE 1826-10/10. Peter the Great's Museum of Anthropology and Ethnography, Leningrad.

Buryat Lamaists used sheep scapulae for divination. The custom entered into the folkways of Lamaism from ancient shamanic traditions of a number of Siberian peoples. The shamans picked the bone clean and threw it into the fire, where it became covered with soot and cracks, the shape and disposition of which was an oracle. The Lamaists wrote a prayer on the bone to increase its effectiveness.

Horn. Metal. Nineteenth century, Buryats. 50 centimeters long. MAE 4692-162. Peter the Great's Museum of Anthropology and Ethnography, Leningrad.

The metal horn called a *gandan* in Tibetan was used in Lamaist temple services. It emitted a harsh sound meant to scare off demons—it is decorated with a depiction of the mouth of a demon who appears to be disgorging both the horn and its sounds.

BOTTOM

Horn. Bone, cloth. Nineteenth century, Buryats. 35 centimeters long. MAE 4698-328. Peter the Great's Museum of Anthropology and Ethnography, Leningrad.

The horn made from a human femur (*ganlin* in Tibetan) was used in tantric Lamaist rituals. To fulfill its function properly, the instrument had to be made from the femur of a virgin. The lama who blew the horn also carried out the magic rite of eating a piece of skin and bone; otherwise the instrument would not sound loudly enough to summon demons.

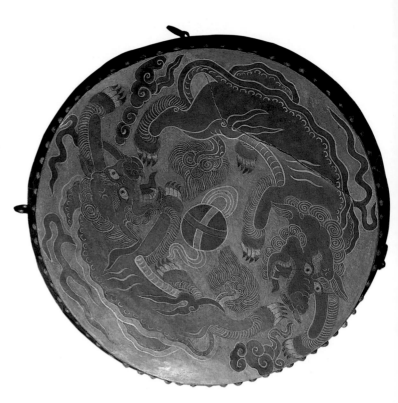

wheel, the swastika, etc.), are actually much older than Buddhism (and thus also Lamaism) and were familiar much earlier both in Indian and central Asian tradition.

It was not only peoples converted to the Lamaist faith who kept alive vestiges of the old local religions. Retention of previous faiths and cults in societies that had accepted new religions is a well-known phenomenon in the history of human culture, and the nomads are no exception. Among the nomads (and settled peoples as well) the major religions could not totally supplant customary beliefs and rituals of previous times. Wherever Christianity came to the nomads, the population as a rule clearly recognized the incompatibility of the old cults and the new religion, although they often continued to resort to traditional religious practices. Among converted Khakass in the early twentieth century, for example, before the shaman began his pagan rites, Christian icons were taken out of the dwelling or turned to the wall, and it was impossible to recite a Christian prayer while the rite was in progress.

Things were quite different among the nomadic Muslims of the same period of time. By that era the most obvious manifestations of paganism were gone, and the pre-Islamic beliefs and rites preserved in popular tradition were perceived as an integral part of Islam but were reinterpreted in Islamic terms. For instance, at the beginning of the twentieth century the magic powers of the sheep's ulna—an ancient Kazakh amulet—were connected with its similarity in shape to the Arab letter *alif.* The Kazakh, Uzbek, and Turkmenian shamans carried out their rites with appeals to Allah and calls for aid to Muslim saints. Some shamans used prayer-beads or the Koran for prophesy or healing instead of the traditional religious objects (drum, whip, etc). And among the Buryats and Tuvinians, shamanism took on some of the ideas and traditions of Lamaism.

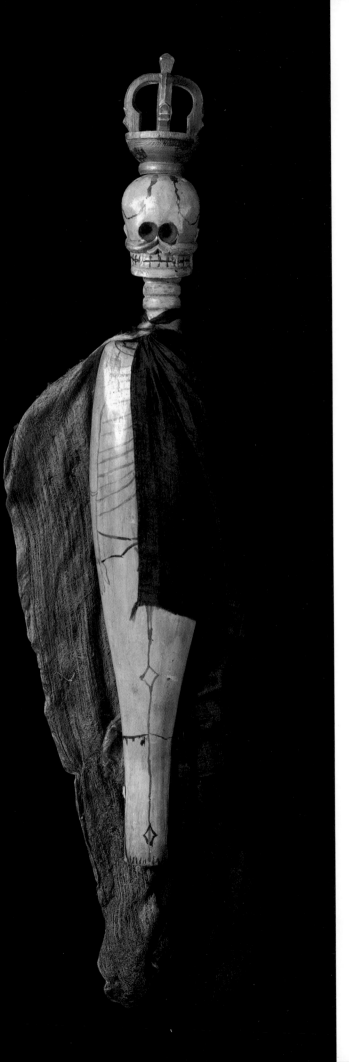

Ceremonial staff model. Wood. Nineteenth century, Buryats. 63 centimeters long. MAE 913-94-16p. Peter the Great's Museum of Anthropology and Ethnography, Leningrad.

The wood model of a staff was used during the Lamaist festival Cham (Buryat: Tsam), a procession of people clad in masks and costumes representing deities and other personages from Buddhist cult and mythology. The costumes were supplemented by wood copies of the ritual attributes of the characters portrayed.

OPPOSITE

Mandala. Metal. Nineteenth century, Buryats. 47.5 centimeters in diameter. MAE 4698-177. Peter the Great's Museum of Anthropology and Ethnography, Leningrad.

The mandala is a sacred symbol, a ritual object in Buddhism. The Sanskrit word signifies circle, disk, sphere, circumference, wheel, territory, part of the Rgveda, etc.; in Buddhism mandala can denote a representation of the universe, a dish for the collection of offerings in temples, or a single image in honor of the gods and the higher lamas. The most widespread interpretation of the mandala is as a model of the universe based on the circle and the square.

In Tibetan Lamaism, and consequently in Mongolia as well, the mandala is perceived as a dwelling place for deities. In the eighth century Padmasambhava, the founder of tantric Buddhism, built the first mandala and then prayed for seven days until a deity descended into its center. During meditation the mandala has the function of aiding the meditator to merge with the cosmic absolute. Some scholars have compared the mandala to the Siberian shaman's drum, which also bears drawings representing the universe.

TOP

Masks. Papier-mâché. Late nineteenth century, Mongols. 35 by 36 and 41 by 40 centimeters. MAE 542-4, 589-7. Peter the Great's Museum of Anthropology and Ethnography, Leningrad.

These masks from the Lamaist Cham festival depict heroes of Buddhist myths. As A. M. Pozdneev wrote, Cham "is held to keep creatures with evil intentions away from the followers of the Buddhist faith by demonstrating the clear presence of the deity on earth to all enemies of faith and virtue." Cham played an important role in establishing Lamaist philosophy and ethical principles among the Mongols and Buryats and acquainting them with tantric Buddhism.

BOTTOM

Cham figures. Wood. 18–20 centimeters high. MAE 327/1–20. Peter the Great's Museum of Anthropology and Ethnography, Leningrad.

Peoples of central Asia celebrated Cham in their temples once a year. In costumes and masks, the lamas performed ceremonial dances to music from religious instruments and enacted scenes from the lives of gods and mortal heroes. There were 108 characters in the classic Cham, each with his own mask and costume, and the color and pomp of the staging attracted huge crowds of believers. Monasteries celebrated Cham in different ways at different times of the year. One scholar, N. N. Shastin, thought that "even the intrinsic content of Cham is different. In general, one should speak not of Cham but of Chams, because there are many of them."

Acronyms of Institutions Lending to the Exhibition

GE   Gosudarstvennyi Ermitazh (Hermitage). Leningrad.

GME   Gosudarstvennyi Muzei Ethnografii Narodov S.S.S.R. (State Museum of Ethnography of the U.S.S.R. Peoples). Leningrad.

IE   Institut etnografii A.N. S.S.S.R. (Institute of Ethnography, U.S.S.R. Academy of Sciences). Moscow-Leningrad.

IIAE   Institut istorii, arkheologii i etnografii A.N. Kazakh S.S.R. (Institute of History, Archaeology, and Ethnography, Kazakh S.S.R. Academy of Sciences). Alma-Ata.

IIFF   Institut istorii, filologii i filosofii Sibirskogo otdeleniya A.N. S.S.S.R. (Institute of History, Philology and Philosophy, Siberian Division, U.S.S.R. Academy of Sciences). Novosibirsk.

MAE   Muzei antropologii i etnografii im. Petra Velikogo (Peter the Great's Museum of Anthropology and Ethnography). Leningrad.

MIRA   Muzei istorii religii i ateizma (Museum of the History of Religion and Atheism). Leningrad.

TRM   Tuvinskii respublikanskii muzei (State Museum of the Tuva A.S.S.R.). Kyzyl.

Contributors

Vladimir Nikolaevich Basilov is editor of *Nomads of Eurasia* and author of several of the essays in the book. Dr. Basilov received his degree in Anthropology in 1967 from the Mikloukho-Maclay Institute of Ethnography in Moscow; he is currently head of the institute's Department of Central Asian and Kazakhstan Research. He has conducted extensive ethnographic field research in Central Asia and published more than 100 papers based on this work.

Mary Fleming Zirin has translated the essays from the Russian. Dr. Zirin, who received her Ph.D. in Slavic Languages and Literature from University of California at Los Angeles in 1971, has lectured and written articles on the Russian language and Russian literary figures. She has translated books and papers on Slavic cultural and scientific topics and is currently completing a dictionary of Russian women writers of the eighteenth and nineteenth centuries.

Vladimir Ivanovich D'yachenko graduated from Leningrad State University in 1980 with a degree in History. He is a specialist in the traditional cultures of the Siberian peoples and is currently Research Associate at the Institute of Ethnography in Leningrad.

Vera Pavlovna D'yakonova is Senior Research Associate in the Section of Ethnography of the Peoples of Siberia, Institute of Ethnography. She graduated with a degree in History from Leningrad State University in 1952; her research interest is the ethnography and archaeology of the peoples of the Sayano-Altai.

Mikhail Viktorovich Gorelik majored in history at Moscow State University and received his degree in 1969. He is Research Associate at the Institute of Oriental Studies in Moscow. His research focuses on weaponry, warfare, and costume of the peoples of the ancient and medieval East.

Mark Grigor'evich Kramarovskii is Curator of the Central Asian Collections of the Hermitage Museum. He received his degree from Ural University in Sverdlovsk in 1969. His special research interest is the history and culture of the Mongolian states of the thirteenth to fifteenth centuries.

Vadim Petrovich Kurylëv, a specialist in the ethnography of Turkic peoples, is Director of the Section of Ethnography of the Peoples of Soviet Central Asia, Kazakhstan, and the Caucasus at the Institute of Ethnography in Leningrad. He received his degree in Oriental Studies at Leningrad State University in 1951.

Nina Petrovna Lobachëva is Senior Research Associate at the Institute of Ethnography in Moscow. She received her degree in Ethnography from Moscow State University and has studied costumes and traditional and new rituals of the peoples of Soviet Central Asia and Kazakhstan.

Evgenii Iosifovich Lubo-Lesnichenko is Director of the Far Eastern Section of the Hermitage Museum. He received his degree in Oriental Studies from Leningrad State University in 1953; his research focuses on the material culture of ancient and early medieval China and the Silk Road.

Ol'ga Borisovna Naumova received her degree in Ethnography from Moscow State University in 1977. She is Junior Research Associate at the Institute of Ethnography in Moscow and a specialist in the ethnic history of the Kazakhs.

Larisa Romanovna Pavlinskaya has a degree in the Theory and History of Art from Repin Institute in Leningrad (1967). She is Research Associate at the Institute of Ethnography in Leningrad and an authority on the traditional culture of the peoples of Siberia.

Georgii Nikolaevich Simakov is a graduate in Oriental Studies of Leningrad State University and Senior Research Associate at the Institute of Ethnography in Leningrad. His research has focused on the social functions of Kirghiz popular pastimes in the late nineteenth and early twentieth centuries.

Sev'yan Izrailevich Vainshtein received his degree in Ethnography from Moscow State University in 1950 and is Honored Scientist of the Tuvinian A.S.S.R. and Research Associate of the Institute of Ethnography in Moscow. He has written over 200 works on aspects of the culture of the people of South Siberia.

Natal'ya L'vovna Zhukovskaya received her degree in History from Moscow State University in 1961; her thesis was on Lamaism and early forms of religion. She is Research Associate at the Institute of Ethnography and author of more than sixty publications on the cultures of the Mongol peoples.

Literature Cited

ABBREVIATIONS:

MIAS   *Materialy i issledovaniya po arkheologii SSSR* [Materials and Research in Soviet Archaeology]

NDIK   *Narodnoe dekorativno-prikladnoe iskusstvo kirgizov. Trudy Kirgizskoi arkheologo-etnograficheskoi ekspeditsii* [Kirghiz Decorative and Applied Folk Art. Works of the Kirghiz Archaeological and Ethnographic Expedition]

SA   *Sovetskaya arkheologiya* [Soviet Archaeology]

SBAE   *Sbornik Muzeya antropologii i etnografii* [Collected Articles of the Museum of Anthropology and Ethnography]

SE   *Sovetskaya etnografiya* [Soviet Ethnography]

Abramson, S. M. 1971. *Kirghizy i ikh etnogeneticheskie i istoriko-kul'turnye svyazi* [The Kirghiz and Their Ethnogenetic and Historic-Cultural Connections]. Leningrad.

Akishev, K. A. 1978. *Kurgan Issyk. Iskusstvo sakov Kazakhstana* [The Issyk Kurgan. The Art of the Sakas of Kazakhstan]. Moscow.

Alektorov, A. E. 1900. Baksa. (Iz mira kirgizskikh sueverii) [Baksa. (From the World of Kirghiz Superstition)]. *Izvestiya Obshchestva arkheologii, istorii i etnografii pri Imperatorskom Kazanskom universitete* [Proceedings of the Kazan' University Archaeological, Historical, and Ethnographic Society] 1.1. Kazan'.

Allworth, E. 1971. *Nationalities of the Soviet East: Publications and Writing Systems. A Bibliographical Dictionary and Transliteration Tables for Iranian- and Turkic-Language Publications, 1818–1945, Located in U. S. Libraries* Columbia University Press.

Ammianus Marcellinus. 1939. *Rerum Gestarum* 3. John C. Rolphe, tr. Cambridge, Mass.: Harvard University Press.

Antipina, K. I. and E. I. Makhova. 1968. *Bezvorsovoe uzornoe tkachestvo* [Flat Patterned Weaving]. *NDIK* 5. Moscow.

Artamonov, M. I. 1961. Antropomorfnye bozhestva v religii Skifov [Anthropomorphic Deities in the Religion of the Scythians]. *Arkheologicheskii sbornik Gosudarstvennogo Ermitazha* [Collected Articles on Archaeology of the Hermitage Museum] 2. Leningrad.

———. 1962. Istoriya khazar [History of the Khazars]. Leningrad.

———. 1973. *Sokrovishcha sakov* [Sakian Treasures]. Moscow.

Atlas. 1961. *Istoriko-etnograficheskii atlas Sibiri* [Historic-Ethnographic Atlas of Siberia]. M. G. Levin and L. P. Potapov, eds. Moscow-Leningrad.

Bartol'd [Barthold], V. V. 1964. Musul'manskie izvestiya o Chingizidakh-Khristianakh [Moslem Sources on Chingisid Christians]. *Sochineniya* [Works] 2.2

———. 1968. Kypchaki [The Kypchaks]. *Sochineniya* [Works] 5.

Basilov, V. N. 1984. *Izbranniki dukhov* [Chosen by the Spirits]. Moscow.

Bichurin, N. Ya. 1950. *Sobranie svedenii o narodakh, obitavshikh v Srednei Azii v drevnie vremena* [Collected Reports on Peoples Who Inhabited Turkestan in Ancient Times] 1. Leningrad.

Chernenko, E. V. 1968. *Skifskii dospekh* [Scythian Armor]. Kiev.

Davydova, A. V. 1985. *Ivolginskii kompleks (gorodishche i mogil'nik)–pamyatnik khunnu v Zabaikal'e* [The Ivolginsk Complex (Settlement and Burial Ground)–A Hunnic Monument in the Transbaikal Region]. Leningrad.

Devlet, M. A. 1976. *Bol'shaya Boyarskaya pisanitsa* [Big Boyarskaya pisanitsa]. Moscow.

Diodorus of Sicily. 1935. C. H. Oldfather, tr. Cambridge, Mass.: Harvard University Press.

Dolukhanov, P. I. 1987. Aridnaya zona Starogo Sveta: Ekologicheskii potentsial i napravlennost' kulturno-khozyaistvennogo razvitiya [The Arid Zone of the Old World: Ecological Potential and the Trend in Culturo-Economic Development]. *Vzaimodeistvie kochevykh kul'tur i drevnikh tsivilizatsii. Tezisy dokladov sovetsko-frantsuzskogo simpoziuma po arkheologii Tsentral'noi Azii i sosednikh regionov* [The Interaction of Nomadic Cultures and Ancient Civilizations. Reports of the Franco-Soviet Symposium on the Archeology of Central Asia and Neighboring Areas]. Alma-Ata.

Dunlop, D. M. 1967. *The History of the Jewish Khazars*. N.Y.: Schocken Books.

D'yakonov, I. M. 1956. *Istoriya Midii* [The History of Media]. Moscow-Leningrad.

Dyrenkova, N. P. 1949. Materialy po shamanstvu u Teleutov. [Material on shamanism among the Teleuts]. *SBEA* 10.

Egami, Namio. 1963. The Economic Activities of the Hsueng-nu. *Trudy XXV Mezhdunarodnogo kongressa vostokovedov* [Proceedings of the XXV Congress of Orientalists] 5. Moscow.

Emsheimer, E. 1943. Preliminary Remarks on Mongolian Music and Instruments. *The Music of the Mongols. Part I. Eastern Mongolia. Reports from the Scientific Expedition to the Northwestern Provinces of China under the Leadership of Dr. Sven Hedin.* Publication 21. Stockholm.

Encyclopedia. 1987. *Encyclopedia of Religion* 15. Mircea Eliade, ed. N.Y.: MacMillan.

Evtyukhova, L. A. 1952. Kamennye izvayaniya Iuzhnoi Sibiri i Mongolii [Stone Statues of South Siberia and Mongolia]. *MIAS* 24.

Fedorov-Davydov, G. A. 1976. *Iskusstvo kochevnikov i Zolotoi ordy* [The Art of the Nomads and the Golden Horde]. Moscow.

———. 1984. *Stadte der Goldenen Horde an der unter Wolga.* Munchen.

Gafferberg, E. G. 1948. Zhilizhche dzhemshidov Kushkinskogo raiona (K istorii zhilishcha kochevnikov) [The Dwellings of the Jamshids of the Kushka Region]. *SE* 4.

———. 1953. Khazareiskaya yurta khonai khyrga (K voprosu ob istorii zhilizhcha kochevnikov) [Afghan Khazar Yurts (The Problem of the History of Nomad Dwellings)]. *SBEA* 14.

Gavrilova, A. A. 1965. *Mogil'nik Kudyrge kak istochnik po istorii altaiskikh plemen* [The Kudyrge Burial as a Source for the History of Altaian Tribes]. Moscow-Leningrad.

Golden, P. B. 1980. *Khazar Studies. A Historico-Philological Inquiry into the Origins of the Khazars.* Budapest.

Golubovskii, P. 1884. *Pechenegi, tyurki, polovtsy do nashestviya tatar* [Pechenegs, Turks, Polovtsians Before the Tatar Invasion]. Kiev.

Gorelik, M. V. 1987. Sakskii dospekh [Sakian Armor]. *Tsentral'naya Aziya. Novye pamyatniki pis'mennosti i iskusstva* [Central Asia. New Monuments of Writing Systems and Art]. Moscow.

Grach, A. D. 1961. *Drevnetyurkskie izvayaniya Tuvy* [Ancient Turkic Statues in Tuva]. Moscow.

———. 1980. *Drevnie kochevniki v tsentre Azii* [Ancient Nomads in the Heart of Asia]. Moscow.

Grakov, B. N. 1971. *Skify. Nauchno-populyarnyi ocherk* [The Scythians. A Popular Essay]. Moscow.

Grigor'ev, A. P. 1981. Offitsial'nyi yazyk Zolotoi ordy XIII–XIV vv. [The Official Language of the Golden Horde of the 13th–14th cc.]. *Tyurkologicheskii sbornik. 1977* Moscow.

Grousset, Rene. 1967. *Conqueror of the World.* Marian MacKellar, tr.; Denis Sinor, preface, notes and tr. Edinburgh: Oliver & Boyd.

Gryaznov, M. P. 1980. *Arzhan* [Arzhan]. Leningrad.

Gumilev, L. N. 1960. *Khunnu. Sredinnaya Aziya v drevnie yremena* [The Khunnu. Turkestan in Ancient Times]. Moscow.

————. 1967. *Drevnie Tyurki* [The Ancient Turks]. Moscow.

Hennig, Richard. 1953. *Terrae Incognitae.* 2d ed. Leiden: E. J. Brill.

Herodotus. 1987. *The History.* David Grene, tr. Chicago: University of Chicago Press.

Hudud al-'Alam. 1937. *Hudud al-'Alam. 'The Regions of the World.' A Persian Geography. 372 A.H.–982 A.D.* V. Minorsky, tr. and notes. V. V. Barthold, preface (tr. from Russian). London: Luzac & Co.

Hughes, Andrew, ed. 1954. *New Oxford History of Music. II. Early Medieval Music up to 1300.* London.

Ibn Battuta. 1929. *Travels in Asia and Africa 1325–1354.* H. A. R. Gibb, tr. London: George Routledge & Sons, Ltd.

Ibn Fadlan. 1939 (1966). *Reisebericht.* Leipzig: Deutsche Morgenländische Gesellschaft (reprint: Nendeln, Liechtenstein: Kraus Reprint Ltd.).

Istoriya Sibiri. 1968. *Istoriya Sibiri s drevneishikh vremen do nashikh dnei* [The History of Siberia from Ancient Times to Our Day] 1. Leningrad.

Istoriya Tuvy. 1964. *Istoriya Tuvy* [The History of Tuva] 1. Kyzyl.

Ivanov, V. V. 1983. *Istoriya slavyanskikh i balkanskikh nazvanii metallov* [The History of Slavic and Balkan Names for Metals]. Moscow.

Jordanes. 1915 (1966). *The Gothic History.* C. C. Mierow, tr., intro. and notes. Cambridge: Speculum Historiale.

Karmysheva, B. Kh. 1956. Zhilishche uzbekov plemeni karluk yuzhnykh raionov Tadzhikistana i Uzbekistana [The Dwellings of the Karluk Tribe of Uzbeks of the Southern Regions of Tadzhikistan and Uzbekistan]. *Izvestiya Akademii nauk Tadzhikskoi SSR. Otdelenie obshchestvennykh nauk* [Proceedings of the Tadzhik SSR Academy of Sciences. Social Sciences] 10–11. Stalinabad.

————. 1980. Kochevaya step' Maverranakhra [The Nomadic Steppes of Transoxiana]. *SE* 1.

————. 1985. Yurta v sovremennom bytu uzbekov. Mastera ee ubranstvo. [The Yurt in Contemporary Uzbek Life. Masters of its Appointments]. *Narodnye mastera. Traditsii. Shkoly* [Folk Craftspeople. Traditions and Schools] 1. Moscow.

Khudyakov, Yu. S. 1982. *Kyrghyzy na Tabate* [The Kirghiz on the Tabat River]. Novosibirsk.

Kirpichnikov, A. N. 1966. *Drevnerusskoe oruzhie. I. Mechi i sabli. IX–XIII vv.* [Old Russian Weapons. I. Swords and sabers. 9th–13th cc.]. Moscow-Leningrad.

Kiselev, S. V. 1950. *Drevnyaya istoriya Yuzhnoi Sibiri* [The Ancient History of South Siberia]. Moscow.

Klyashtornyi, S. G. 1964. *Drevnetyurkskie runicheskie pamyatniki kak istochnik po istorii Srednei Azii* [Old Turkic Runic Texts as a Source for the History of Turkestan]. Moscow.

————. 1965. Problemy rannei istorii plemen turk (ashina) [Problems of the Early History of the Turkic Tribes (A-shih-na)] *Novoe v sovetskoi arkheologii* [New Findings in Soviet Archaeology]. Moscow.

Kokovtsev, P. K. 1932. *Evreisko-khazarskaya perepiska v X v.* Moscow.

Konovalov, P. V. 1976. *Khunnu v Zabaikal'e* [The Khunnu in the Transbaikal Region]. Ulan-Ude.

Kovalevskaya, V. B. 1977. *Kon' i vsadnik* [Horse and Rider]. Moscow.

Kramarovskii, M. G. 1973. In: V. F. Gening and M. G. Kramarovskii. *Ivdel'skaia nakhodka* [A Find at Ivdel']. Leningrad.

————. 1985. Serebro Levanta i khudozhestvennyi metall Severnogo Prichernomor'ya XIII-XV vv. [Levantine Silver and the Art Metalwork of the Regions North of the Black Sea in the 13th and 14th cc.]. *Khudozhestvennye pamyatniki i problemy kul'tury Vostoka* [Eastern Artistic Monuments and Cultural Questions of the East. Leningrad.

Ksenofontov, G. V. 1929. *Kul't sumasshestviya u uralo-altaiskom shamanisme* [The Cult of Madness in Ural-Altaic Shamanism]. Irkutsk.

Kubarev, V. D. 1984. *Drevnetyurkskie izvayaniya Altaya* [Ancient Turkic Statues of the Altai]. Novosibirsk.

Kuz'mina, E. E. 1977. Rasprostranenie konevodstva i kul't konya u iranoyazychnykh plemen Srednei Azii i drugikh narodov Starogo Sveta [The Spread of Horse-Breeding and the Cult of the Horse among the Iranic-Speaking Tribes of Turkestan and Other Peoples of the Old World]. *Srednyaya Aziya v drevnosti i srednevekov'e (istoriya i kul'tura)* [Turkestan in Ancient Times and the Middle Ages (History and Culture)]. Moscow.

Kuz'mina, E. E., and V. A. Lifshits. 1987. Eshche raz o proiskhozhdenii yurty [Another Round on the Origin of the Yurt]. *Proshloe srednei Azii* [The Past in Turkestan]. Dushanbe.

K-v, A. 1903. Tainstvennaya tamga [A Mysterious Brand]. *Turgaiskaya gazeta* 15–16.

Laszlo, G. 1974. *Steppenvolker und Germanen.* Berlin.

Levshin, A. 1832. Opisanie kirgiz-kazachskikh ili kirgis-kaisakskikh ord i stepei [Description of the Kirghiz-Kazakh or Kirgis-Kaisa Hordes and Steppes]. *Etnograficheskie opisaniya* [Ethnographic Descriptions] 3. St. Petersburg.

Liu Mau-Tsai. 1958. *Die chinesischen Nachrichten zur Geschichte der Ost-Turken (T'u-kue)* 1. Wiesbaden.

Lubo-Lesnichenko, E. I. 1969. Kitaiskie lakovie izdeliya iz Noin-Uly [Chinese Lacquerware from Noin-Ula]. *Trudy Gosudarstvennogo Ermitzha* [Works of the Hermitage (Museum)] 10.

Maenchen-Helfen, J. Otto. 1973. *The World of the Huns. Studies in Their History and Culture.* Max Knight, ed. Berkeley, Calif.: University of California Press.

Makhova, E. I. and N. V. Cherkasova. 1968. Ornamentirovannye izdeliya iz voiloka [Decorated Felt Articles]. *NDIK* 6. Moscow.

Malov, S. E. 1951. *Pamyatniki drevnetyurkskoi pis'mennosti. Teksty i issledovaniya* [Monuments of Old Turkic Writing. Texts and Studies]. Moscow-Leningrad.

Mansurova, V. I. 1979. *Angliiskie srednevekovye istochniki IX–XIII vv. Kliment Aleksandriiskii* [English Medieval Sources of the 9th–13th cc. Clement of Alexandria] 4. Moscow.

Margulan, A. Kh. 1964. Kazakhskaya yurta i ee ubranstvo [The Kazakh Yurt and Its Appointments]. (Doklad na VII Mezhdunarodnom kongresse antropologicheskikh i etnograficheskikh nauk) [Paper Read at the 7th International Anthropological and Ethnographic Congress]. Moscow.

Markov, G. E. 1976. *Kochevniki Azii* [Nomads of Asia]. Moscow.

Masanov, E. A. 1959. Kazakhskoe voiloch-noe proizvodstvo vo vtoroi polovine XIX i nachale XX vekov [Kazakh Felt Production of the Second Half of the 19th and Beginning of the 20th cc.]. *Trudy Instituta istorii, arkheologii i etnografiya AN Kazakh SSR* [Works of the Institute of History, Archaeology and Ethnography of the AS Kazakh SSR] 6. Alma-Ata.

[Masanov, E. A.] 1966. *Ocherki istorii etnograficheskogo izucheniya kazakh-skogo naroda v SSSR* [Sketches of the History of Ethnographic Studies of the Kazakh People in the USSR]. Alma-Ata.

Moshkova, V. G. 1946. Plemennye "goli" v turkmenskikh kovrakh. [Tribal "goli" in Turkmenian carpets]. *SE* 1.

————. 1970. *Kovry narodov Srednei Azii kontsa XIX–nachala XX vekov. Materialy ekspeditsii 1929–45 gg.* [Carpets of the Peoples of Turkestan of the Late 19th–Early 20th cc. Materials of the 1929–1945 Expeditions]. Tashkent.

Mukanov, M. S. 1979. *Kazakhskie domashnie khudozhestvennye remesla* [Kazakh Domestic Arts and Crafts]. Alma-Ata.

————. 1981. *Kazakhskaya yurta* [The Kazakh Yurt]. Alma-Ata.

Narody Sibiri. 1956. *Narody Sibiri* [The Peoples of Siberia]. M. G. Lcvin and L. P. Potapova, eds. Moscow.

Narody Srednei Azii. 1962, 1963. *Narody Srednei Azii i Kazakhstana* [Peoples of Soviet Central Asia and Kazakhstan]. 2 vols. S. P. Tolstov et al., eds. Moscow.

Okladnikov, A. P. 1940. K voprosu o proiskhozhdenii i meste luka v istorii kul'tury [The Problem of the Origin and Place of the Bow in the History of Culture]. *Kratkie soobshcheniya Instituta istorii material'noi kul'tury* [Short Reports of the Institute for the History of Material Culture] 5.

Pallas, P. S. 1776 [1967]. *Reise durch verschiedene Provinzen des Russischen Reichs* 3. Graz, Austria: Akademische Druck- u. Verlagsanstalt [reprint].

Pan Ku. 1935. *Ch'ien Han shu.* Shanghai. In translation: *The History of the Former Han Dynasty.* 3 vols. Homer H. Dubs,s tr. Baltimore: Waverley Press 1938.

Plano Carpini, John of. 1955. History of the Mongols. *The Mongol Mission: Narratives and Letters of the Franciscan Missionaries in Mongolia and China in the Thirteenth and Fourteenth Centuries.* Christopher Dawson, ed. and intro. A Nun of Stanbrook Abbey, tr. London: Sheed and Ward. 3–76.

Pletneva, S. A. 1958. Pechenegi, tyurki, polovtsy v yuzhnorusskikh stepyakh [Pechenegs, Turks, and Polovtsians in the South Russian Steppes]. *MIAS* 62.

———. 1976. *Khazary* [The Khazars]. Moscow

Pliny the Elder. 1947. *Natural History* 2. H. Rackham, tr. Cambridge, Mass.: Harvard University Press.

Polo, Marco. 1984. *Travels.* Teresa Waugh, ed. Maria Bellonci, tr. Great Britain: Sidgwick and Jackson. N.Y.: Facts on File Publications.

Polyak, A. N. 1964. Novye arabskie materialy pozdnego srednekov'ya o Vostochnoi i Tsentral'noi Evrope [New Arab Materials on the Late Middle Ages in East and Central Europe]. *Vostochnye istochniki po istorii narodov Yugo-Vostochnoi i Tsentral'noi Evrope* [Eastern Sources on the History of the Peoples of Southeast and Central Europe]. Moscow.

Poppe, N. N. 1941. Zolotoordynskaya rukopis' na bereste [A Golden Horde Manuscript on Birchbark]. *Sovetskoe vostokovedenie* [Soviet Oriental Studies] 2. Moscow-Leningrad.

Potapov, I. A. 1972. *Yakutskaya narodnaya rez'ba po derevu* [Yakut Folk Woodcarving]. Yakutsk.

Pritsak, O. 1978. The Khazar Kingdom: Conversion to Judaism. *Harvard Ukrainian Studies* 2. Cambridge, Mass.: Harvard Ukrainian Research Institute.

Radloff, W. 1884. *Aus Sibirien. Lose Blätter aus dem Tagebuche eines reisenden Linguisten.* 2 vols. Leipzig.

Raevskii, D. S. 1977. *Ocherki ideologii skifo-sakskikh plemen* [Sketches on the Ideology of the Scytho-Sakian Tribes]. Moscow.

Rakhmatullin, K. A. 1968. Tvorchestvo manaschi. [The Work of the Manaschi (Kirghiz bards)] *Manas–geroicheskii epos kirgizskogo naroda* [Manas–Heroic Epic of the Kirghiz People]. Frunze.

Rashid ad-Din. 1952, 1960. *Sbornik letopisei* [Collected Manuscripts] 1 and 2. Moscow-Leningrad.

Rostovtsev, M. I. 1925. *Skifiya i Bospor* [Scythia and the Bosphorus]. Petrograd.

Rubruck, William of. 1955. Journey. *The Mongol Mission.* Christopher Dawson, ed. and intro. London: Sheed and Ward. pp. 89–220.

Rudenko, S. I. 1953. *Kul'tura naseleniya Gornogo Altaya v skifskoe vremya* [The Culture of the Population of the Altai Mountains in Scythian Times]. Moscow-Leningrad. In translation as: *Frozen Tombs of Siberia.* M. W. Thompson, tr. and preface. Berkeley, Calif.: University of California Press, 1970.

———. 1962. *Kul'tura gunnov i noin-ulinskie kurgany* [The Culture of the Huns and the Noin-Ula Kurgans]. Moscow-Leningrad.

———. 1968. *Drevneishie v mire khudozhestvennye kovry i tkani iz oledenelykh kurganov Gornogo Altaya* [The Most Ancient Artistic Carpets and Fabrics in the World from the Frozen Kurgans of the Altai Mountains]. Moscow.

Sachs, Curt. 1940. *The History of Musical Instruments.* N.Y.: Norton.

Sel-skomu uchitelyu. 1983. *Sel'skomu uchitel'yu o narodnykh khudozhestvennykh promyslakh Sibiri i Dal'nego Vostoka* [To A Village School Teacher about the Folk Crafts of Siberia and the Far East]. Moscow.

Sher, Ya. A. 1966. *Kamennye izvayaniya Semirech'ya* [Stone Statues of the Semirech'e Region]. Moscow-Leningrad.

Shvetsov, M. L. 1979. "Polovetskie svyatilishcha" [Polovtsian Sacred Places]. *SE* 1.

Smirnov, A. P. 1957. O pogrebeniyakh s konem i truposozhzheniyakh epokhi bronzy v Nizhnem Povolzh'e [Burials with a Steed and Cremations in the Bronze Age on the Lower Volga]. *SA.*

Smirnov, K. F. 1984. *Sarmaty i utverzhdenie ikh politicheskogo gospodstva v Skifii* [The Sarmatians and Their Establishment of Political Dominion in Scythia]. Moscow.

Ssu-ma Ch'ien. 1961. *Records of the Grand Historian of China* 2. Burton Watson, tr. N.Y.: Columbia University Press.

Stebleva, I. V. 1965. *Poeziya Tyurkov VI–VIII vv.* [Turkic Poetry of the VI–VII cc.]. Moscow.

Struve, V. V. 1968. Pokhod Dariya I na sakov-massagetov [The Campaign of Darius I Against the Saka-Massagetae]. *Etiudy po istorii Prichernomor'ya, Kavkaza i Srednei Azii* [Studies in the History of the Black Sea Region, Caucasus and Turkestan]. Leningrad.

Sukhareva, O. A. 1960. *Islam v Uzbekistan* [Islam in Uzbekistan]. Tashkent.

———. 1979. Opyt analiza pokroev traditsionnoi "tunikoobraznoi" sredneaziatskoi odezhdy v plane ikh istorii i evolyutsii. [Historical and Evolutionary Analysis of the Styles of the Traditional "Tuniclike Cut" of Soviet Central Asian Clothing] *Kostium narodov Srednei Azii. Istoriko-etnograficheskie ocherki* [The Costume of the Peoples of Soviet Central Asia. Historical-Ethnographic Sketches]. Moscow.

Sychev, V. L. 1977. Iz istorii plechevoi odezhdoi narodov Tsentral'noi i Vostochnoi Azii (K probleme klassifikatsii) [The History of the Upper Garments of Central and East Asia (Classification Problems)]. *SE* 3.

Tokarev, S. A. 1936. *Dokapitalisticheskie perezhitki v Oirotiya* [Precapitalist Survivals in Oirotia]. Leningrad.

———. 1958. *Etnografiya narodov SSSR* [Ethnography of the Peoples of the USSR]. Moscow.

Tolstov, S. P. 1947. Goroda guzov [Cities of the Guz]. *SE* 3.

———. 1948. *Drevnii Khorezm* [Ancient Khorezm]. Moscow.

———. 1958. Khorezmskaya arkheologo-etnograficheskaya ekspeditsiya [Archeological-Ethnographic Expedition to Khorezm]. *SE* 1.

al 'Umari, Ibn Fadl Allah. 1968. *Das Mongolische Weltreich. Al 'Umari's Darstellung der Mongolischen Reiche in seinem Werk Masalik al-absar fi mamalik al-amsar.* Klaus Lech, tr. and ed. Wiesbaden: Otto Harrassowitz.

Vainshtein, S. I. 1958. Osedlye poseleniya i oboronitel'nye sooruzheniya v Tuve [Sedentary Settlements and Defensive Works in Tuve]. *Uchenye zapiski Tuvinskogo nauchno-issledovatel'skogo instituta yazyka, literatury i istorii* [Notes of the Tuvinian Institute of Languages, Literature, and History] 8 (Kyzyl).

———. 1964. Drevnii Por-Vazhin [Ancient Por-Vazhin]. *SE* 6.

———. 1966. Nekotorye voprosy istorii drevnetyurkskoi kul'tury [Problems of the History of Ancient Turkic Culture]. *SE* 3.

———. 1972. *Istoricheskaya etnografiya tuvintsev* [Historical Ethnography of the Tuvinians]. Moscow. In English as: *Nomads of South Siberia.* Caroline Humphrey, ed. and intro. Cambridge: Cambridge University Press, 1980.

———. 1976. Problemy istorii zhilishcha stepnykh kochevnikov Evrazii [Problems in the History of the Dwellings of the Steppe Nomads of Eurasia]. *SE* 4.

———. 1980. Fenomen muzykal'nogo iskusstva, rozhdennyi v stepyakh [A Phenomenon of Musical Art Born on the Steppes]. *SE* 1.

Vainshtein, S. I., and V. A. Korenyako. 1988. O genezise iskusstva kochevnikov: Avary [The Genesis of Nomad Art: The Avars]. *Narody Azii i Afriki* [Peoples of Asia and Africa] 1.

Vainshtein, S. I., and M. V. Kryukov. 1966. Ob oblike drevnikh tyurkov [What the Ancient Turks Looked Like], *Tyurkologicheskii sbornik* [Collected Articles on Turkology]. Moscow.

———. 1985. Sedlo i stremya [Saddle and stirrup]. *Znanie* [Knowledge]. April 1985.

Valikhanov, Ch. Ch. 1985. Vooruzhenie kirghiz v drevnie vremena i ikh voennye dospekhi [Kirghiz Weaponry in Ancient Times and Their Martial Armor]. *Sobranie sochinenii* [Collected Works] 4. Alma-Ata.

Vasil'ev, D. L. 1983. *Korpus tyurkskikh runicheskikh pamyatnikov basseina Eniseya* [The Corpus of Turkic Runic Monuments in the Enisei Basin]. Leningrad.

Vasil'eva, G. P. 1979. Nekotorye tendentsii razvitiya sovremennykh natsional'nykh traditsii v material'noi kul'ture narodov Srednei Azii i Kazakhstana [Some Tendencies in the Development of Contemporary National Traditions in the Material Culture of the Peoples of Soviet Central Asia and Kazakhstan]. *SE* 3.

———. 1984. Materialy po zhilishchu turkmen Tashauzskoi i Chardzhouskoi oblastei [Materials on the Dwellings of the Turkmens of Tashauz and Chardzhou Regions]. *Polevye issledovaniya Instituta Etnografii 1980–1981* [Field Work of the Ethnographic Institute: 1980–1981]. Moscow.

———. 1985. Uzornye voiloki turkmenskikh masterits [Patterned Felts by Turkmenian Craftswomen. *Narodnye mastera. Traditsii, shkoly* [Folk Craftworkers. Traditions and Schools] 1. Moscow.

Zagryazhskii, G. S. 1874. Byt kochevogo naseleniya dolin Chu i Syrdar'i [The Daily Life of the Nomadic Population of the Chu and Syrdar'ya Valleys]. *Turkestanskie vedomosti* [Turkestan Gazette] 29, 30.

Zakhoder, B. N. 1967. Shirazskii kupets v Povolzh'e v 1438 g. [A Merchant from Shiraz in the Volga Region in 1438]. *Kaspiiskii svod svedenii o Vostochnoi Evrope* [The Caspian Collection of Reports on Eastern Europe] 2. Moscow.

Zhdanko, T. A. 1961. Problema poluosedlogo naseleniya v istorii Srednei Azii i Kazakhstana [The Problem of Seminomadic Populations in the History of Turkestan and Kazakhstan]. *SE* 2.

Zhirmunskii, V. M. 1974. *Tyurkskii geroicheskii epos* [The Old Turkic Heroic Epos]. Leningrad.

Zolotarev, A. M. 1964. *Rodovoi stroi i pervobytnaya mifologiya* [The Clan System and Primeval Mythology]. Moscow.

Additional Literature

Agadzhanov, S. G. *Ocherki istorii Oguzov i Turkmen Srednei Asii IX–XIII vv.* [Sketches from the History of the Oghuz and Turkmenians of Turkestan in the 9th to 13th cc.]. Ashkhabad 1969.

Akishev, A. K. *Iskusstvo i mifologiya sakov* [Art and Mythology of the Sakas]. Alma-Ata 1984.

Alekseev, N. A. *Traditsionnye religioznye verovaniya yakutov v XIX–nachale XX v.* [Traditional Yakut Religious Beliefs in the 19th to Early 20th cc.]. Novosibirsk 1975.

Bachmann, Werner. *The Origins of Bowing and the Development of Bowed Instruments up to the Thirteenth Century.* Norma Deane, tr. London: Oxford University Press 1969.

Barber, E. J. W. *Prehistoric Textiles.* Princeton, N.J.: Princeton University Press. In press.

Bessonova, S. S. *Religioznye predstavleniya naseleniya stepnoi Skifii* [Religious Concepts of the Population of the Scythian Steppes]. Kiev 1979.

Chernikov, S. S. *Zagadka zolotogo kurgana* [Enigma of the Golden Kurgan]. Moscow 1965.

Devlet, M. A. Pamyatniki skifskogo vremeni v Severo-Vostochnoi Tuve [Monuments from Scythian Times in Northeast Tuva]. *Pervobytnaya arkheologiya Sibiri* [Primitive Archaeology of Siberia]. Leningrad 1975.

Dioszegi, Vilmos. *Tracing Shamans in Siberia.* A. R. Babo, tr. Oosterhout: Anthropological Publications 1968.

Egorov, V. L. *Istoricheskaya geografiya Zolotoi Ordy v XIII–XIV vv.* [Historical Geography of the Golden Horde in the 13th–14th cc.] Moscow 1985.

El'nitskii, L. A. *Skifiya evrasiiskikh stepei* [Scythia of the Eurasian Steppes]. Novosibirsk 1977.

Erdniev, U. E. *Kalmyki* [Kalmyks]. Elista 1970.

Etnicheskie problemy Tsentral'noi Azii v drevnosti [Ethnic Problems of Ancient Central Asia]. M. S. Asimov et al., eds. Moscow 1981.

Etnografiya karakalpakov. XIX–nachalo XX veka. Materialy i issledovaniya [Ethnography of the Karakalpaks. 19th and Early 20th c. Materials and Studies]. Tashkent 1980.

Fedorov-Davydov, G. A. *Kochevniki vostochnoi Evropy pod vlast'yu Zolotoordynskikh khanov* [Nomads of East Europe under the Power of the Khans of the Golden Horde]. Moscow.

From the Lands of the Scythians. Ancient Treasures from the Museums of the U.S.S.R. 3000 B.C.–100 B.C. N.Y.: Metropolitan Museum of Art; Los Angeles: Los Angeles County Museum of Art. N.Y.: New York Graphic Society 1976.

Gorelik, M. V. Rannii mongol'skii dospekh [Early Mongol Armor]. *Arkheologiya, etnografiya i antropologiya Mongolii* [Archaeology, ethnography and anthropology of Mongolia]. Novosibirsk 1987.

Gryaznov, M. P. Tagarskaya kul'tura [The Tagar Culture]. *Istoriya Sibiri* [History of Siberia] 1. Leningrad 1968.

Halperin, Charles J. *Russia and the Golden Horde.* Bloomington: Indiana University Press 1965.

Heissig, Walther. *The Religions of Mongolia.* Geoffrey Samuel, tr. from German. London: Routledge & Kegan Paul 1980.

Istoriya Yakutskoi ASSR [History of the Yakut ASSR] 2. Moscow-Leningrad 1957.

Khazanov, A. M. *Sotsial'naya istoriya skifov (Osnovnye problemy razvitiya drevnikh kochevnikov evraziiskikh stepei)* [Social History of the Scythians (Basic Problems of the Development of the Ancient Nomads of the Eurasian Steppes)]. Moscow 1975.

———. *Nomads and the Outside World.* Julia Crookenden, tr. Ernst Gellner, foreword. Cambridge University Press 1984.

Khristianstvo i lamaism u korennogo naseleniya Sibiri [Christianity and Lamaism among the Native Population of Siberia]. Leningrad 1979.

Kniga moego deda Korkuta [Book of My Grandfather Korkut]. Moscow 1962.

Konstantinov, I. V. *Material'naya kul'tura Yakutov XVIII veka* [Material Culture of the Yakuts in the 18th c.] Yakutsk 1971.

Kubarev, V. D. *Drevnie izvayaniya Altaya. Olennye Kamni* [Ancient Altaian Sculptures. Deer Stones]. Novosibirsk 1979.

Kurylëv, V. P. Oruzhie kazakhov [Kazakh Weapons]. *SBEA 34. Material'naya kul'tura i khozyaistvo narodov Kavkaza, Srednei Azii i Kazakhstana* [Collected Articles of the Museum of Anthropology and Ethnography. 34. Material Culture and Economy of the Peoples of the Caucasus, Soviet Central Asia, and Kazakhstan]. Leningrad 1978.

Kwanten, Luc. *Imperial Nomads: A History of Central Asia, 500–1500.* University of Pennsylvania 1979.

Lattimore, Owen. The Geography of Chingis Khan. *Geographical Journal* 1963 129:1.1–27.

Machinskii, D. A. O vremeni pervogo aktivnogo vystupleniya sarmatov v Podneprov'e po svidetel'stvam antichnykh pis'mennykh istochnikov [The Time of the First Active Incursion of the Sarmatians into the Dnepr Region from the Evidence of Ancient Written Sources]. *Arkheologicheskii sbornik Gosudarstvennogo Ermitazha* [Collected Articles on Archaeology of the Hermitage Museum]. 1971.

Mackerras, Colin. *The Uighur Empire (744–840): According to the T'ang Dynastic Histories.* Canberra: Centre of Oriental Studies, Australian National University 1968.

Masanov, E. A. Iz istorii remesla kazakhov [From the History of Kazakh Handicrafts]. *SE* 1958 5.

McGovern, William Montgomery. *The Early Empires of Central Asia: A Study of the Scythians and the Huns and the Part They Played in World History.* Chapel Hill: University of North Carolina Press 1939.

Michael, Henry N., ed. *Studies in Siberian Shamanism.* Toronto: University of Toronto Press 1963.

Morgan, David. *The Mongols.* Oxford: Basil Blackwell 1986.

Moshkova, M. G. *Proiskhozhdenie rannesarmatskoi (prokhorovskoi) kul'tury.* [Origin of the Early Sarmatian (Prokhorovo) Culture]. Moscow 1974.

Narodnoe iskusstvo Yakutii [Folk Art of Yakutia]. Moscow 1971.

Novgorodova, N. A. *Alte Kunst der Mongolei.* Leipzig: Seemann Verlag 1980.

———. *Drevnyaya Mongoliya* [Ancient Mongolia]. Moscow 1988.

Ocherki po istorii khozyaistva narodov Srednei Azii i Kazakhstana (Trudy Instituta etnografii AN SSSR 98) [Sketches from the History of the Economy of the Peoples of Soviet Central Asia and Kazakhstan (Works of the AS USSR Institute of Ethnography 98)]. Leningrad 1973.

Orazov, A. *Etnograficheskie ocherki khozyaistva turkmen Akhala v XIX–nachale XX v.* [Ethnographic Sketches of the Akhal Turkmenians in the 19th and early 20th cc.]. Ashkhabad 1985.

Phillips, E. D. *The Mongols.* N.Y.: Frederick A. Praeger 1969.

———. *The Royal Hordes: Nomad Peoples of the Steppes.* London: Thames and Hudson 1965.

Piotrovskii, B. B. Skify i Drevnii Vostok [The Scythians and the Ancient East]. *SA* 19 (1954).

Potapov, L. P. Obryad ozhivleniya shamanskogo bubna u tyurkoyazychnykh plemen Altaya [The Ritual of Bringing the Shaman's Drum to Life among the Turkic Tribes of the Altai]. *Trudy Instituta etnografii imeni N. N. Miklukho-Maklaya* [Works of the Miklukho-Maklai Institute of Ethnography] 1. Moscow-Leningrad 1947.

———. Drevnii obychai, otrazhayushchii pervobytno-obshchinnyi byt kochevnikov [Ancient Customs Reflecting the Primitive Communal Way of Life of the Nomads]. *Tyurkologicheskii sbornik* [Collected Articles on Turkology] 1. Moscow-Leningrad 1951.

———. *Ocherki narodnogo byta tuvintsev* [Sketches from Tuvinian Traditional Life]. Moscow 1969.

Problemy istorii obshchestvennogo soznaniya aborigenov Sibiri [Problems of the History of the Social Consciousness of the Autochthonous Peoples of Siberia]. Leningrad 1981.

Rashid al-Din. *Successors of Genghis Khan.* John Andrew Boyle, tr. from Persian. N.Y.: Columbia University Press 1971.

Rossabi, Morris. *Khubilai Khan: His Life and Times.* Berkeley: University of California Press 1988.

Rudenko, S. I. *Gornoaltaiskie nakhodki i skify* [Finds in the Altai Mountains and the Scythians]. Moscow-Leningrad 1952.

———. *Bashkiry (Istoriko-etnograficheskie ocherki)* [Bashkirs (Historical-Ethnographic Sketches)]. Moscow-Leningrad 1955.

———. *Kul'tura naseleniya Tsentral'nogo Altaya v skifskoe vremya* [The Culture of the Population of Central Altai in Scythian Times]. Moscow-Leningrad 1960.

Seroshevskii, V. L. *Yakuty. Opyt etnograficheskogo issledovaniya* [Yakuts. An Experiment in Ethnographic Investigation]. St. Petersburg 1896.

Shaniyazov, K. Sh. and Kh. I. Ismailov. *Etnograficheskie ocherki material'noi kul'tury uzbekov kontsa XIX–nachala XX v.* [Ethnographic Sketches of the Material Culture of the Uzbeks in the Late 19th and Early 20th cc.]. Tashkent 1961.

Shramko, B.A. Iz istorii skifskogo vooruzheniya [From the History of Scythian Weaponry]. *Vooruzhenie skifov i sarmatov* [Scythian and Sakian Weaponry]. Kiev 1984.

Smirnov, K. F. *Vooruzhenie sauromatov* [Weapons of the Sauromatae]. Moscow 1961.

———. *Savromaty (Rannyaya istoriya i kul'tura sarmatov)* [Sauromatae (Early History and Culture of the Sarmatians)]. Moscow 1964.

———. *Skify* [Scythians]. Moscow 1966.

———. Savromato-sarmatskii zverinyi stil' [Sauromatian-Sarmatian Wild-Beast Style]. *Skifo-sibirskii zverinyi stil' v iskusstve narodov Evropy* [Scytho-Siberian Wild-Beast Style in the Art of the Peoples of Europe]. Moscow 1976.

Spüler, Bertold. *Die Goldene Horde: die Mongolen in Russland 1223–1502.* 2d ed. Wiesbaden 1965.

Strany i narody. Sovetskii Soyuz. Respubliki Zakavkaz'ya. Respubliki Srednei Azii. Kazakhstan [Lands and Peoples. The Soviet Union. The Transcaucasian Republics. The Republics of Soviet Central Asia. Kazakhstan]. Moscow 1984.

Tolybekov, S. E. *Kochevoe obshchestvo kazakhov v XVII–nachale XX veka* [Nomadic Society of the Kazakhs from the 17th to Early 20th c.]. Alma-Ata 1971.

Trippett, Frank. *The First Horsemen.* N.Y.: Time-Life Books 1974.

Tucci, Giuseppe. *The Religions of Tibet.* Geoffrey Samuel, tr. Berkeley, Calif.: University of California Press 1980.

Vainshtein, S. I. *Istoriya narodnogo iskusstva Tuvy.* Moscow 1974.

Vasil'eva, G. P. Sovremennoe sostoyanie narodnogo dekorativno-prikladnogo iskusstva turkmen [The Contemporary State of Turkmenian Applied Arts]. *SE* 1974 5.

Vladimirtsov, B. Ya. *Obshchestvennyi stroi mongolov* [The Social Structure of the Mongols]. Leningrad 1934.

Volkov, V. V. *Bronzovyi i rannii zheleznyi vek Mongolii* [Bronze and Early Iron Ages in Mongolia]. Ulan-Bator 1967.

Zhdanko, T. A. Nomadism v Srednei Azii i Kazakhstane (Nekotorye istoricheskie i etnograficheskie problemy) [Nomadism in Soviet Central Asia and Kazakhstan (Some Historical and Ethnographic Problems)]. *Istoriya, arkheologiya i etnografiya Srednei Azii* [History, Archaeology and Ethnography of Soviet Central Asia]. Moscow 1968.

Zhebelev, S. A. *Severnoe Prichernomor'e: Issledovaniya i stat'i po istorii Severnogo Prichernomor'ya antichnoi epokhi* [The North Coast of the Black Sea: Studies and Articles on the History of the North Coast of the Black Sea in Ancient Times]. Moscow-Leningrad 1953.

Index

NOMADS OF EURASIA
was produced for the

NATURAL HISTORY MUSEUM OF LOS ANGELES COUNTY
by PERPETUA PRESS, LOS ANGELES

Project Manager: ROBIN A. SIMPSON
Copyeditor: CONNIE SALVETTA
Cartographer: MARTHA BREEN
Indexer: THE INFORMATION BANK

Book Designer: DANA LEVY
Production Coordinator: LETITIA BURNS O'CONNOR
Typeset in Trump Mediaeval by CONTINENTAL TYPOGRAPHICS
Printed by DAI NIPPON PRINTING CO., Tokyo
Printed on U-LITE PAPER